Ernest Rutherford

And the Explosion of Atoms

OXFORD
PORTRAITS
IN SCIENCE

Owen Gingerich
General Editor

Ernest Rutherford

And the Explosion of Atoms

J. L. Heilbron

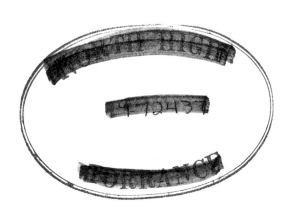

OXFORD
UNIVERSITY PRESS

OXFORD

UNIVERSITY PRESS

Oxford   New York
Auckland   Bangkok   Buenos Aires   Cape Town   Chennai
Dar es Salaam   Delhi   Hong Kong   Istanbul   Karachi   Kolkata
Kuala Lumpur   Madrid   Melbourne   Mexico City   Mumbai   Nairobi
São Paulo   Shanghai   Singapore   Taipei   Tokyo   Toronto

Published by Oxford University Press, Inc.
198 Madison Avenue, New York, New York 10016
www.oup-usa.org

Oxford is a registered trademark of Oxford University Press

Design: Design Oasis
Layout: Lenny Levitsky

Library of Congress Cataloging-in-Publication Data

Heilbron, J. L.
Ernest Rutherford : and the explosion of atoms / John L. Heilbron.
p. cm.—(Oxford portraits in science)
Summary: A biography of the scientist considered to be the father of nuclear physics
for his development of the nuclear theory of the atom in 1911 and discovery of alpha
and beta rays. Includes bibliographical references and index.
ISBN 0-19-512378-6 (acid-free paper)
1. Rutherford, Ernest, 1871-1937--Juvenile literature. 2. Physicists-New Zealand-
Biography-Juvenile literature. 3. Nuclear physics-History-Juvenile literature. [1.
Rutherford, Ernest, 1871-1937. 2. Physicists. 3. Scientists. 4. Nuclear physics-
History. 5. Nobel Prizes-Biography.] I. Title. II. Series.
QC16.R8 H45   2003
539.7'092--dc21   2002155600
Printing number: 9 8 7 6 5 4 3 2 1

Printed in the United States of America
on acid-free paper

On the cover: *Ernest Rutherford;* inset: *Rutherford works in his basement on the
megnetization of iron.*
Frontispiece: *A 1932 portrait of Rutherford by Oswald Birley.*

Contents

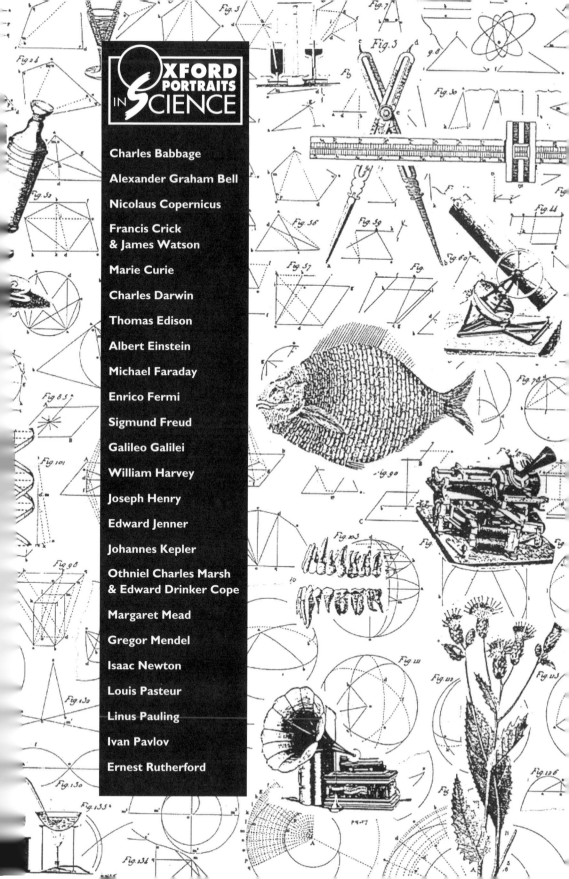

OXFORD PORTRAITS IN SCIENCE

Introduction

The earth's crust and atmosphere have been radioactive since their creation. Human beings knew nothing about the radiations in which they bathed, however, until a hundred years ago, around 1900, when they first made conscious contact with rays from uranium, discovered the apparently inexhaustible radiator known as radium, and invented the concept of radioactivity.

Twenty-five hundred years ago a few Greek philosophers decided that the material world was composed of hard, indestructible particles they called atoms. Their theory, revived in Europe 2,000 years later, set the crucial question for chemistry and physics: Do atoms exist? Radioactivity helped to confirm both their existence and their non-existence by showing that although the atoms that figured in the theories of physics and chemistry did indeed exist, they were not indestructible.

Five hundred years ago western Europe was alive with alchemists, people who believed that base metals could be transmuted into gold. Much time and money were transmuted into nothing in the attempt to demonstrate the theory. The alchemists failed, not because their aims were frivolous, but because transmutation requires much more powerful methods than they had at their disposal. Their failure made "alchemist" a synonym for "imposter." In radioactivity, however, nature itself regularly transmutes one sort of chemical atom into another.

The man who discovered nature's transmutations and the structure of the atom was Ernest Rutherford, whose career is as interesting as the science he advanced. Born the son of a flax farmer in the most remote part of the English-speaking world, he ended up a British baron and the chief professor at the center of the universe of physics. His journey ran from the margin to the interior, from New Zealand to Cambridge, through unexplored worlds where only he could see the direction of advance. Fortunately, the record of his path breaking is intelligible as well as inspirational. Rutherford's science was not mysterious and mathematical like Einstein's or burdened with details like Marie Curie's. It consisted of bold inferences from apt experiments, disciplined common sense, and inspired neglect of what other people thought important.

When, late in life, down-to-earth "Ern" Rutherford transmuted into Lord Rutherford of Nelson, he did not forget his origins. He designed a shield displaying items seldom sighted in the British Isles: a kiwi bird and a Maori warrior. These creatures, intended to refer to the exotic place of his birth, may also be read as indicators of prominent traits in his character. Like the wingless kiwi, Rutherford, a no-nonsense, robust, commonsensical man, had his feet fixed firmly on the ground. Like the Maori warrior, he was always prepared for action against anyone foolish enough to oppose him.

Rutherford became a life peer in 1931. He took as his baronial crest a design indicating his achievements in science (the crossing curves on the shield) and his origins in New Zealand (the kiwi bird on the left and the Maori warrior on the right). The sage on the left, Hermes Trismegistus, represents ancient alchemy; the Latin slogan, "to inquire into the foundations of things," states the enduring quest of physics.

Cambridge and Ray Physics

A little more than a century before Ernest Rutherford's birth on August 30, 1871, Captain James Cook, the great explorer and geographer, made the first extensive survey of the coasts of New Zealand. He landed a few times to repair his ships, restore his crews, acquire food and water, and claim territory for England. The natives with whom he traded—the Maori—teetered between ferocity and friendliness; he thought them very pleasant for cannibals, strong, artistic, ingenious, and brave. But their warlike habits and taste for barbecued sailors discouraged visitors, and it was not until 1840 that missionaries succeeded in gaining a toehold where the Royal Navy had declined to tread. Colonialization, largely from Scotland, followed quickly. Rutherford's grandfather, a wheelwright, was one of the first to land.

By 1870 the islands had an immigrant population of around half a million, about ten times that of the natives. Despite this plentiful supply, the Maori gave up cannibalism. The two races coexisted more peacefully than whites and American Indians in the United States, in large part because land agreements were faithfully kept. The fact that the

Rutherford grew up in this house facing the sea in New Zealand. His father ran the flax mill on the property.

colonists of New Zealand were in the main educated, hard-working folk, and not the adventurers who led European expansion in the western United States, also helps to account for the difference in race relations. The schoolhouse spread through New Zealand as the saloon did through the American West.

Rutherford's mother was a schoolteacher. The family numbered 14, Ern being the fourth of 12 children. They lived outside the little port of Nelson (population around 5,000) at the north end of the South Island. Rutherford's first home perched on the slope of a river valley; later, when his father took up flax farming, the family moved to a place near the swamp where the flax plant thrived. Rutherford

Rutherford's parents, James and Martha, photographed around 1880.

grew up in pioneering country, hunting and fishing in forests and streams, able to make and repair the tools necessary to maintain a civilized life in a remote village, pressed by his mother to keep up his studies, and exposed to a sober but not severe religious and moral training. He emerged a clever teenager, cheerful and strong, with a good earthy sense of humor, no airs, a wide set of manual skills, no obvious genius, an indifference to religion, and, despite having many sisters, a remarkable shyness with girls.

At the age of 15 Rutherford won a scholarship to Nelson College, a high school with 80 students, all boys. His father took him by horseback over the mountains from the flax farm to the tiny town where the college was located. Rutherford did very well in all his subjects, Latin, English, French, and especially mathematics; he left high school able to write good economical English, to read French easily, and to handle trigonometry. During his last year, he was the "Dux," or head boy; fortunately his scholarship brought him money prizes as well as reputation, since his family's resources would not otherwise have allowed him to board at the college. His outstanding performance was the result of quick comprehension aided by special coaching in mathematics and an enviable ability, acquired in the din at home, to concentrate on the task at hand whatever the disturbances and temptations around him.

The promising head boy won a scholarship to study at University College in Canterbury, a town many times larger than Nelson. He continued at Latin and English—he was a gluttonous reader all his life, especially of detective stories and the novels of Dickens—but concentrated on physics and mathematics. Once again a stream of scholarships and prizes kept his body and soul together while his mind absorbed everything presented to it. He graduated with a "double first"—an A+—in physics and astronomy.

What next? Rutherford had arrived at the top of the educational ladder in New Zealand. He was good at many subjects. He particularly enjoyed the laboratory work he had done during his last years at Canterbury. It had resulted in a modest invention, a new type of receiver for radio waves. The receiver looked promising and important: radio waves were then newly discovered (the first intentional production of them took place in 1887) and the means of detecting them were very primitive. Despite the importance and promise of his invention, however, Rutherford did not have the resources or the time to develop it in New Zealand. He had to earn his way as soon as he could. His feeling of urgency was the doing of Mary Newton, known in her family as May to distinguish her from her mother, also named Mary, a redoubtable fighter for temperance and women's rights. Rutherford became acquainted with the Newtons as their lodger during his time at Canterbury. They had been forced to let rooms when Mary's husband left them (by drinking himself to death) to fend for themselves. Ern and May, then still in her teens, become engaged but—we are still in Victorian times—they agreed not to marry until Rutherford had the means to support a family.

An obvious choice of career was medicine. Rutherford regarded it unenthusiastically. Nor did farming appeal to him. In 1894, when at the age of 23 he was still hesitating over his vocation, he learned that New Zealand's turn had come to nominate a candidate for an "exhibition" to study abroad. This exhibition, one of the fellowships endowed by the International Exhibition of Arts and Sciences held in London in 1851, was shared in rotation by Australia and New Zealand. Rutherford applied. He failed. The judges in London preferred a chemist from Auckland. Rutherford fell back on teaching physics in high school, a job he disliked.

During the summer, as he was digging potatoes on his father's farm and worrying about how to continue the work he liked, earn a living, and marry Mary, his mother brought him a telegram. It was the offer of the exhibition. His rival the chemist had renounced it for marriage and a stable job.

Rutherford had no problem postponing his wedding. He threw down his spade. "That's the last potato I'll dig," he is to have said as he packed his bags for Europe.

The overseas exhibitioner could take his scholarship wherever he pleased. Rutherford thought at first he would go to Germany, where radio waves had been discovered; but before he came to a decision, their discoverer, Heinrich Hertz, had died, and Hermann von Helmholtz (Hertz's teacher) and other prominent German physicists had also passed away. Germany was not so lively as Rutherford had first thought. He switched his attention to the Cavendish Laboratory of Cambridge University. By a stroke of good fortune, the opportunity to do research there had just been opened to aliens—that is, to people who had not obtained their bachelor's degree at Cambridge. This uncharacteristi-

Rutherford measures the level of the soaking pond of his family's flax mill. The soaking rots the outer stem of the flax, which is stripped off to free the inner fibers. The fibers may then be combed and spun into rope or fabric.

cally generous act, which many old-fashioned dons opposed, immediately had one of the consequences they feared. It turned the Cavendish Laboratory almost overnight from a teaching institution with a few slow investigators into the most important and dynamic research school in physics in the world.

The opening of closeted Cambridge allowed the Cavendish to recruit advanced students who could support themselves. The number of researchers went from 5 in 1894 to 30 at the end of the century; only one-third of these had Cambridge bachelor's degrees. The influx increased quality as well as quantity. The first year's crop—those who came in

Rutherford's fiancée, Mary Newton, in 1896, about the time of her engagement.

with Rutherford in 1895—included another future Nobel prize–winner, Charles Thomson Rees Wilson, several future professors, and Paul Langevin, who became one of France's most important physicists, a life-long friend of Rutherford, and, more briefly, the lover of Mme Curie.

The head of this research group was Joseph John ("J. J.") Thomson, a clever mathematician and ingenious designer of experiments, which, because he tended to break things in the laboratory, were usually done by someone else. A shrewd judge of talent and character, and already distinguished for his work on electricity and magnetism, Thomson was just under 40 and (as Rutherford wrote to Mary, evidently in surprise) "not fossilized at all. . . . He is a medium sized man, dark and quite youthful still, shaves very badly and wears his hair rather long." Thus Rutherford described to his fiancée the unkempt man who would be his mentor, become his friend, and launch his career. He needed the support Thomson gave, especially during his first few months, when the native demonstrators (teaching assistants) sneered at the barbaric newcomers without Cambridge degrees. Rutherford had a suitably barbaric response. "There is one demonstrator on whose chest I would like to dance a Maori war dance."

At Thomson's urging, Rutherford joined a college, which made him a regular undergraduate as well as a research student. The connection gave him social and intellectual support. A college in Oxford or Cambridge is a hall of residence offering instruction and affiliated with the university. In Rutherford's time the affiliation was loose: the colleges, some very rich, ran their own affairs and their heads, acting as a body, tended to run the university. Besides undergraduates, who paid fees, the colleges had senior residents, including several sorts of fellows. These might be tutors or lecturers in the college, professors in the university, administrators, or holders of prize fellowships that gave them room, board, and spending money for one or several years while they pursued research projects or higher degrees. Most of the money for the prize fellowships came from the college's own funds. When Rutherford arrived in Cambridge in 1895, there were relatively few prize fellowships in science.

Trinity was the most open to mathematics and science of all the Cambridge colleges. Thomson belonged to it and Rutherford followed his lead—after Thomson had persuaded the governing body to reduce the fees for research students. Still, the expense told and to economize Rutherford rented a room outside the college and usually ate what his landlady provided.

Having made himself as comfortable as possible, Rutherford returned to his detector. In January 1896 he managed to detect radio waves at a distance of 100 feet, across three thick stone walls. With Thomson's encouragement, he planned to try for half a mile. He succeeded in this, the longest transmission yet achieved anywhere, on leap day 1896. He gave demonstrations all over Cambridge and also in London, dining out frequently as the man from New Zealand who could push electricity through stone walls.

He was not at ease at the more elaborate of these dinner parties. The gowns worn by the ladies shocked his prudish rustic sensibility. "Some of the dresses were very décolleté," Rutherford wrote Mary after dining with some underdressed women. "I must say I don't admire it at all. Mrs X., wife of a professor, wore a 'creation'. . . bare arms right up to the shoulder and the rest to match. I wouldn't like any wife of mine to appear so, and I'm sure you wouldn't either." He had nothing to fear on that score; Mary had been brought up opposed to tobacco, alcohol, and low-cut dresses.

Thomson urged Rutherford to consider commercial development of the radio detector, but nothing came of it. His financial resources and opportunities had scarcely improved.

text continues on page 21

CATHODE RAY TUBES

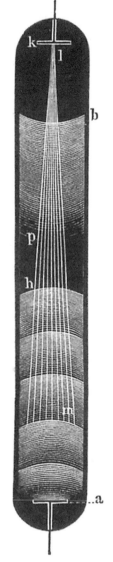

Only a highly charged body can send a spark across a wide expanse of normal air. The most spectacular example is a lightning flash between an electrified cloud and the oppositely electrified earth beneath it. But if air or other gases are enclosed in a glass tube furnished with electrodes (electrical plates that can be charged up like the cloud and the earth), sparks and other glows can be obtained with more modest means than nature uses to make lightning. All that is necessary is to pump out some of the gas in the tube. When the pressure falls low enough, pleasant glows in striking colors fill the vessel.

In explanation, physicists say that the electric field between the electrodes accelerates the ions (charged particles) naturally present in a gas; that these ions acquire enough speed before striking the residual gas molecules to be able to ionize them; and that the ions thus produced, making others in the same way, create enough charged particles to carry a current and to give off visible light. The partial but not complete vacuum is essential to allow ions enough room to pick up substantial speeds under the electric force before colliding with, and losing their energy to, gas molecules. The light arises from the energy radiated during the recombination of ions into neutral atoms or molecules.

The shape, color, and number of the striations in a dilute gas depend on the nature of the conductors through which electricity enters and leaves the gas (electrodes), the kind of gas, and the degree of vacuum. Here k signifies the cathode (the entrance or negative electrode), the lines lm the invisible cathode rays, a the anode (the exit or positive electrode), the space between h and a the "positive glow," and the space between b and p the "negative glow."

continues on page 20

continued from page 19

The light dies out as the pressure is diminished further until, in the best vacuums available in the later 19th century, the tube does not flash when the current passes. In compensation, a patch of glass directly opposite the cathode (the negative electrode) fluoresces with an eerie pale green light. Physicists supposed that an unknown radiation, originating at the cathode and travelling in straight lines from it, caused the fluorescence. They called this hypothetical radiation "cathode rays" and tried in vain to identify them with the physical agents they knew. J. J. Thomson discovered that they were streams of charged particles much smaller in size than the atoms of ordinary matter. He called them corpuscles. They are known today as electrons.

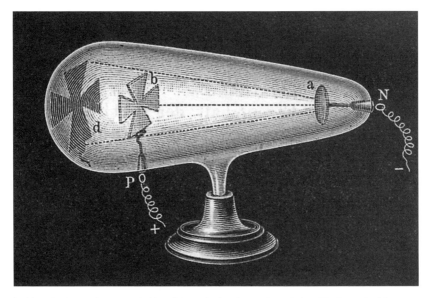

In this cathode-ray tube, a metal object (b) attached to the anode and placed in the path of the rays from the cathode (a) cast a shadow (d) on the fluorescent patch made by the rays where they strike the glass walls of the tube.

text continued from page 18

Until his last year at Cambridge, when he had an unusual third year as an exhibitioner and a valuable Cambridge fellowship, Rutherford was always on the verge of insolvency. He set aside his detector to work with Thomson on another sort of radiation capable of penetrating opaque bodies but much easier to detect and study than radio waves.

This extraordinary agent, called X rays by their discoverer, Wilhelm Conrad Roentgen, and roentgen rays by almost everyone else, revealed itself to mankind during Rutherford's first Christmas at Cambridge in 1895. Physicists returning to their laboratories after the holidays found in their mailboxes a printed pamphlet that contained a report on the properties of the rays and a photograph of the inside of Frau Roentgen's living hand. The physicists were flabbergasted. Most of them had the apparatus needed to produce the rays and the photographic equipment to detect them; but no one had noticed them before or could account for them now.

Among the possibilities aired was that the production of X rays resembled fluorescence—the property some minerals have of shining in the dark for a time after being illuminated by ordinary light. The idea of a connection with fluorescence arose from the observation that the rays seemed to come from a bright green fluorescent patch on the glass of the tube that produced them. The pursuit of this idea, which turned out to be altogether wrong, resulted in a second discovery (X rays being the first) of capital importance. As Columbus discovered long ago, when he found America while looking for Asia, wrong reasoning can bring you to the right place.

The Columbus who sought X rays in fluorescence was Henri Becquerel, a physicist with a scientific pedigree of three generations. His grandfather had acquired a professorship in Paris early in the 19th century; Becquerel II, Henri's father, succeeded to this professorship, to which he added another; Henri got both posts, and a third as well. In

France an enterprising professor could accumulate academic posts and hold them all simultaneously, which substantially reduced the number of professors and usefully increased their incomes.

Among the items of scientific interest passed down among the Becquerels was a beautiful fluorescing crystal that contained uranium. Becquerel exposed this beauty to sunlight to excite its fluorescence, set it on a wrapped pho-

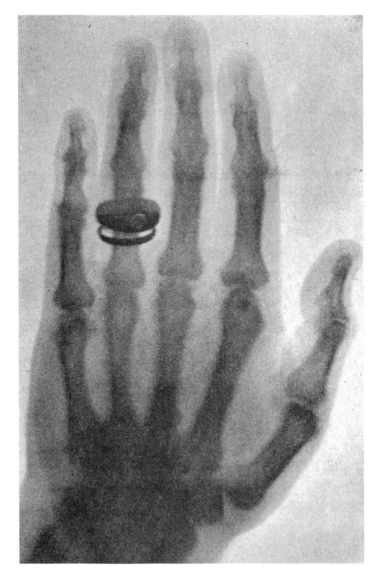

The eerie half-transparent hand quickly became the icon of W. C. Roentgen's discovery of X rays. The hand in this X-ray photograph belonged to the anatomist Rudolf Albert von Koelliker, Röntgen's colleague at the University of Würzburg and a founder of the Physical-Medical Society to which Röentgen announced his discovery.

tographic plate, and shut the crystal and the plate in a drawer to test whether it gave rise to non-visible rays capable of penetrating the wrapping. It did. A second trial gave a similar result. Then came a day when the sun did not shine in Paris. Nonetheless, the plate darkened through its wrapping. The crystal required no stimulation to produce penetrating rays! Apparently uranium or some other constituent of the crystal possessed the ability to radiate spontaneously. Becquerel presented this insight to the Paris Academy of Sciences in May 1896.

Meanwhile, in Cambridge, Thomson and Rutherford found that roentgen rays have a peculiar effect on gases. A gas ordinarily does not conduct electricity. Immediately after irradiation by X rays, however, it can pass an electrical current easily. The sketch, in Rutherford's hand, of the apparatus they used to find and demonstrate this effect, is reproduced on the following page. Thomson and Rutherford explained that an X ray striking a gas molecule

The physics research group at the Cavendish Laboratory, Cambridge, in 1898, included J. J. Thomson (seated in the middle of the first row with his arms across his chest), Rutherford (standing just behind Thomson), C. T. R. Wilson (standing to Rutherford's right), and Paul Langevin (seated to Thomson's right).

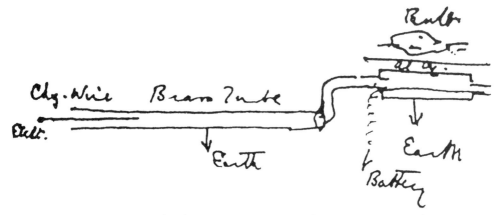

A sketch, in Rutherford's
typically illegible hand, of
the apparatus with which
he and J. J. Thomson dis-
covered that X rays can
ionize gases. The rays,
produced in the bulb at
the upper right, make
positive ions in air flowing
into the chamber
beneath the bulb. The
ions deposit their electricity on the negatively
charged wire at the far
left, which is attached to
an electrometer. The
downward arrows indi-
cate that the brass tube
containing the air flow is
grounded.

can divide it into a positive and a negative part. These parts are called "ions" after a Greek word meaning "to go," since they can move through the gas under electrical forces. The ability to create ions became an important laboratory test: Rays that do not ionize the air cannot be X rays.

An obvious question for the physicist of 1896 was whether the rays that Becquerel had found in uranium were X rays. Rutherford showed that uranium rays ionize air and so might be X rays, and that, whatever Becquerel's rays might be, they consisted of two quite distinct types. One type, which he called alpha, made many ions, but did not penetrate far through matter; a few thin sheets of aluminum absorbed alpha rays almost entirely. The other type, beta, ionized lightly and penetrated further. The study of the rays from radioactive substances, especially the alpha fraction, was to engage Rutherford for most of his research career and inspire his greatest discoveries.

By the time Rutherford's fellowship expired in the summer of 1898, European physicists had found several sub-stances that radiated like uranium. The leader in the search was a woman as strong-willed as Rutherford. Maria Skladowska, the daughter of a schoolteacher, was 28 in 1895, when she married a physics professor named Pierre Curie. She was then a student at the University of Paris, one of the few institutions in Europe at which a woman could earn a doctor's degree. For her thesis project, she used an electrical method similar to Rutherford's to show that a certain uranium ore called pitchblende was three or four times as "radioactive" (to use the word she coined) than uranium. She reasoned that pitchblende must contain a strong radiator and she had a ton or so of it dumped at Pierre's laboratory in Paris.

Together, Marie and Pierre Curie tore the ore apart chemically, testing every component for radioactivity and analyzing still further the fractions that displayed it. One fraction was 400 times more active than uranium. They called the unknown and otherwise undetectable radioactive agent in this fraction "polonium" after Marie's native country, Poland. The Curies announced their discovery of polonium in July 1898, just as Rutherford finished his analysis of the rays from uranium. By the following Christmas the Curies had found a radioactive substance carried along with barium in their chemical processes. They purified this substance as well as they could and, early in 1899, had a sample of it no less than 100,000 times more active than uranium. They called it "radium" and expected that, like polonium, it would turn out to be a new element. Marie's isolation of minute quantities of radium confirmed their expectation.

Radium immediately captured the public imagination. Like X rays, it was a subject of wonder in an age not yet jaded with wonders. And like X rays, it seemed providently provided to help cure the ills of the 20th century. Both were used to treat cancer and skin problems, often doing equal damage to doctor and patient. But whereas X rays could be generated cheaply and plentifully with everyday apparatus and immediately found widespread use as a diagnostic tool, radium was a scarce and expensive chemical product applied mainly to burning out serious tumors. Its cost, driven up by medical demand, made it difficult to procure in quantity for physical experiments. A lucky few, among them Rutherford, received specimens as gifts from Marie Curie.

The world of physics was fuller in 1898 than it had been a decade earlier. Beginning with the first generation and detection of radio waves by Hertz in 1887, physicists had uncovered a series of natural agents astonishing in their power and properties. After a few years of experimenting with the passage of electricity through gases, they had recognized the existence of gaseous ions and had defined "cathode rays," the hitherto unknown cause of the fluorescence of the glass opposite the cathode in an evacuated glass vessel passing an electric current. It was while preparing to study cathode rays that Roentgen discovered X rays and while following a false analogy between X radiation and fluorescence that Becquerel discovered uranium rays. The activity of uranium gave rise, on the one hand, to the activity of the Curies, who found two new elements, polonium and radium, by concentrating the carriers of the radioactivity of pitchblende; and, on the other hand, to the activity of Rutherford, who found two different sorts of rays, alpha and beta, in the radiation from uranium. Only three years elapsed between the great gifts of Christmas 1895 and Christmas 1898, between X rays and radium.

But that was not all, or even the principal part, of the physical discoveries of the late 1890s. When Rutherford went his own way with uranium rays, Thomson turned to the question of the nature of the cathode rays. At the time, two opinions were current among the physicists of Europe. One, held primarily by Germans, likened cathode rays to light; the other, pushed by the English, likened them to charged particles. The question came down to this: Could the rays be bent by electric and magnetic forces? If so, the English position would be strengthened, since electromagnetic forces do not alter the direction of light rays. In 1895 the evidence for the theories seemed to be evenly balanced: Cathode rays could be bent by a magnetic force but not, apparently, by an electric one.

In 1897 Thomson succeeded in forcing cathode rays to bend to electricity. By placing electrodes within a cathode-ray tube from which most of the air had been pumped out, he could make the fluorescent patch on the glass, which indicated the presence of cathode rays there, move up and down under electric forces. He succeeded where others had failed by imagining himself sitting on a cathode ray and dodging the "jolly little beggars," to use Rutherford's pet name for ions, in his path. Having succeeded in moving the fluorescent spot both electrically and magnetically, Thomson adjusted the strength of the two forces until the rays traveled in a straight line. Knowing the strength of the forces in play when they exactly counterbalanced and assuming that the cathode-ray particles acted like minute balls of mass m carrying an electric charge e, Thomson had just enough information to deduce a value for the ratio e/m, but not for e or m separately. The size of this ratio, e/m, amazed everyone competent to have an opinion on the subject. It came out about 1,000 times larger than the same ratio for the ion of hydrogen, the lightest element known.

If the e/m of the "corpuscle," as Thomson renamed the cathode ray particle, is a thousand times that of the hydrogen ion, then either the corpuscle's charge e is much larger than the ion's, and/or its mass m is much smaller. Thomson made the bold and shrewd guess that the charges are the same and, moreover, the smallest charges in nature. It followed that the hydrogen ion outweighed the corpuscle a thousand-fold. And furthermore, adding guess to guess, Thomson conjectured that the corpuscle, which he had detected only in cathode rays, was a universal building block of matter. Indeed, he supposed it to be the only building block, the only sort of material body in the universe. He saw everything, even the hydrogen atom, as a vast collection of corpuscles. That was certainly to overplay his hand. There are things in atoms besides corpuscles. Rutherford was to find them.

text continues on page 29

MEASURING THE *E/M* OF THE CORPUSCLE

Thomson first measured the *e/m* of the corpuscle with this glass apparatus. Rays from the cathode at C, accelerated through the metal napkin rings A and B, curve when the metal plates D and E are connected through a powerful battery (not shown). By adjusting the electric force between D and E so as to cancel the deflection caused by a magnetic field across the tube, Thomson could determine the rays' velocity. With that he could work out *e/m* from the magnetic or electric bending alone.

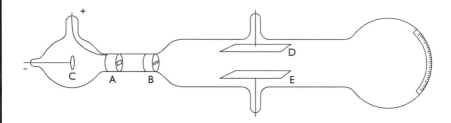

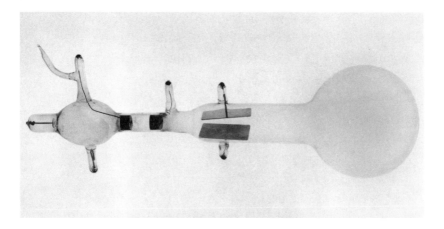

text continued from page 27

The oddest thing about Thomson's far-fetched conjectures is that by 1900 most physicists had accepted most of them as correct. Much of the supporting evidence was assembled at the Cavendish Laboratory by the barbarous research students without Cambridge degrees. A key step was the measurement of *e*. To make it, Thomson exploited the knowledge, which he had from Rutherford's fellow student C. T. R. Wilson, that ions can act as centers for the formation of water droplets in a fog. Passing X rays through humid air to create the ions, Thomson made a large number, *N* say, of droplets; if the charge on each of the ions, and hence on each droplet, is *e*, then if all the droplets fall on a detector of electricity, it should record a total charge of *Ne*. By weighing all the droplets, Thomson could deduce a value for *N* and thus for *e*. The corpuscle's charge came out close to the known charge on the hydrogen ion. That gained the important point that the corpuscle's mass was very small, about a billionth of a billionth of a billionth of a gram, to be almost precise.

That did not bridge the huge gap between Thomson's analysis of cathode rays and his claim that corpuscles make up everything. But soon particles with the same value of e/m as the corpuscle's turned up in many different experimental situations in many different laboratories. A most telling case was found by two Dutch physicists, Pieter Zeeman (an experimentalist a few years older than Rutherford) and his professor, Hendrik Antoon Lorentz (the leading theoretical physicist in Europe). They explained the emission of light by atoms as a consequence of the rapid

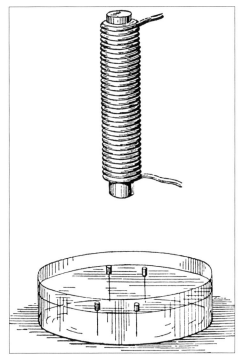

Thomson's magnetic analogy to the electronic structure of atoms. The big vertical electromagnetic pole plays the part of the atom's positive charge; the floating corks, with their vertical magnetic needles, that of the atomic electrons. The analogy suggested that electrons could arrange themselves in concentric circles under the influence of electrical forces alone.

motions of corpuscle-like particles within them. In another striking instance, Becquerel showed that beta rays were not X rays but fast cathode rays. Thomson reasoned from the Dutch experiments that corpuscles were constituents of normal atoms and, from Becquerel's, that they must also be parts of radioactive ones.

Thomson's TOE (or Theory of Everything, to use the phrase with which modern theoretical physicists modestly specify their objective) would have been incomplete without an indication of how thousands of corpuscles can constitute atoms and give them their particular chemical properties. Thomson did not falter. He supposed that when many corpuscles congregate in a very small space, the space acts as if it contained just enough positive charge to neutralize them and hold them together as an atom. He then allowed the corpuscles to rotate in concentric rings within their atom and supposed that the number and populations of the rings determined the atom's chemical properties and the sort of light (the spectrum) it emitted. Thomson was to devote much of his time during the decade after the discovery of the corpuscle to making this picture plausible.

Picture making of this type did not impress European physicists like the Curies, who regarded it as childish, arbitrary, and English. British physicists thought it the glory of their science. James Clerk Maxwell, the first Cavendish professor and the greatest British physicist of the 19th century, had recommended the "robust form and vivid colouring of a physical illustration," that is, of a picturable model like Thomson's atom. Lord Kelvin, who invented the absolute scale of temperature, laid the first telegraph cable under the Atlantic Ocean, and contributed something to all branches of the physics of his time, went further. He could not reason, he said, without making a visualizable picture, or mechanical model, of the phenomenon he wanted to explain.

In a speech delivered in 1895, the German chemist Wilhelm Ostwald, who did not believe in atoms, decried the British love of explicit pictures or physical models and admonished them in the words of scripture, "thou shalt not take unto thee any graven image or any likeness of anything." He was answered by an Irish physicist, George Francis Fitzgerald; doing without images, said Fitzgerald, "might be all right for a German, who plods by instinct, but a Briton wants emotion in his science, something to raise enthusiasm, something with human interest," that is, a full-bodied, imaginative, imaginary model.

The recognition that the model did not exist literally in nature was essential to its success. Thomson did not care what mode of picture making his students adopted; he insisted only that they use at least one. Hence, perhaps, his extraordinary success as a teacher: he trained seven Nobel prize winners, 27 fellows of the Royal Society (the most prestigious honorific organization of British science), and dozens of professors. Rutherford took from Thomson not only an understanding of physics and the power of a strong group of graduate students, but also the methods and goals of English modeling and the peculiar problem of the structure of the atom.

McGill and the Explosion of Atoms

"Rejoice with me, my dear girl, for matrimony is looming in the distance." With these words, written while working on his paper on uranium rays, Rutherford announced to Mary Nelson that, at his first try and with J. J.'s strong endorsement, he had been offered a professorship. It paid 500 pounds a year, more than three times as much as his exhibition, and was enough for a young couple to live on in a modest way. He had been very worried about his financial future because opposition from the old dons to the new postgraduate research men made him doubt his prospects for continuing support at Cambridge beyond 1898: "I know perfectly well that if I had gone through the regular [under-graduate] Cambridge course, and done a third of what I have done, I would have got a [college] Fellowship bang off." Now however, he no longer had to distress himself over local prejudices.

The only negative aspect of his chair was its location thousands of miles from Cambridge, at McGill University

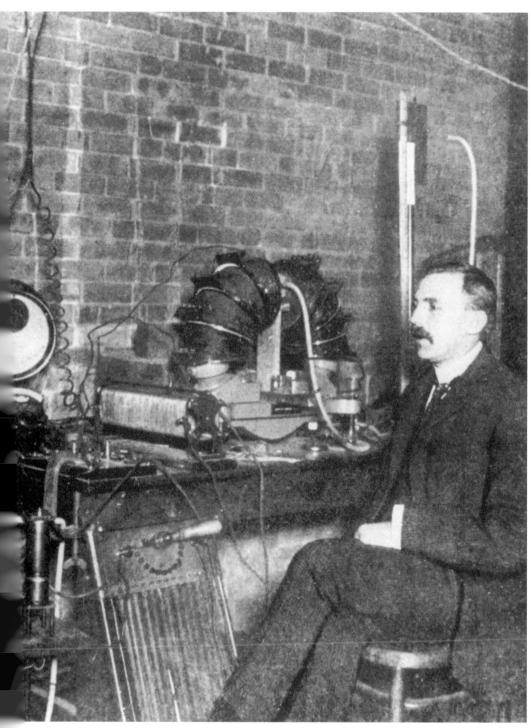

Rutherford sits at a small workbench in his laboratory at McGill University; the bench supports the entire apparatus for an experiment on rays from radioactive substances. The suit was not Rutherford's normal laboratory garb; a newspaper photographer took this picture for an article on radioactivity written in 1905.

in Montreal, Canada. In compensation for the distance, he was offered all the resources necessary to perform wonders. He explained his task to Mary: "I am expected to do a lot of original work and to form a research school in order to knock the shine out of the Yankees." He had four weeks or so to complete his work in Cambridge, write it up, pack, and catch the boat for Canada. He treated himself to a first-class ticket, not yet having to economize to support a wife. Rutherford planned to labor hard setting up at McGill through the academic year and then, the following summer (that would be 1899), sail off to New Zealand to claim his bride. In the event, he found Montreal too expensive, and himself too poor, to fetch her then. He decided to save half his salary for two years as a nest egg before tearing himself from his laboratory long enough to return home for the first time in five years and marry his patient Mary.

Although unusually young for a professor (he was just 27), Rutherford expected to be "practically boss man in the laboratory." Officially, the boss was John Cox, a Cambridge man with little taste for research, who gave his junior colleagues free access to the extraordinary resources under his control. The physics building was the most costly and probably the largest one in the world when it opened in 1893. It was a present to McGill from the university's greatest patron, William MacDonald, a parsimonious teetotalling anti-smoker who had grown rich selling cigarettes to his fellow citizens. He spared no expense, except on himself. "Let us have everything of the best," he had told Cox, who had asked for five thousand pounds for equipment. MacDonald gave six thousand, equivalent to perhaps a million dollars today, and also provided funds for assistants, maintenance, and mechanics. Even 100 years ago you could not do physics without money. MacDonald's generosity enabled Rutherford not only to outshine the Yankees but also to outdo all the physicists and chemists of Europe despite the handicap of working far from the major centers of science.

Rutherford's predecessor at McGill, a Cambridge man named Hugh Callendar, was a careful experimenter who made heat measurements applicable to steam turbines and car motors. His brand of physics appealed to the practically minded Canadians who doubted that anyone so fine could be found to replace him. "I think my appointment is a very much discussed matter," Rutherford wrote Mary, "as Callendar was considered a very great man. Your acute mind will at once gauge my importance if they place me in his shoes when the beard of manhood is faint upon my cheeks." Rutherford had no intention of becoming another Callendar, however. "I don't quite class myself in the same order as Callendar, who was more an engineering type than a physicist, and who took more pride in making a piece of apparatus than in discovering a new scientific truth." In 1900 he showed the class he was in by discovering, as he put it to Mary with becoming modesty, "1000 new facts which have been undreamt of."

The facts emerged in the course of Rutherford's routine project of examining the rays from the element thorium, which Marie Curie and others had shown to be radioactive, in the same way that he had probed the rays of uranium. Not expecting to find much, Rutherford gave the project to the MacDonald professor of electrical engineering, R. B. Owens, who had wanted to learn something about radioactivity. Owens found that, like uranium, thorium gave out both alpha and beta rays. But he was not happy about the experiment because the rays seemed to respond to Rutherford's presence in the laboratory. How did Rutherford do it? He did not know. Together, Owens and Rutherford traced Rutherford's odd power over the rays to air currents set up when he opened or closed the laboratory door.

What was the air blowing about? Vapor of thorium? Unknown ions? Not knowing, Rutherford gave the agent the vague label "emanation," indicating thereby a ghostly, mysterious, but substantial presence. He led this ghost down a long glass tube and learned that it was radioactive, although in a way grossly different from thorium, uranium, polonium, and radium. Whereas their activity seemed inexhaustible, the emanation's fell to half strength in a minute. Moreover, the walls of the tube became radioactive where the emanation touched them. Like the emanation, the "induced activity" on the walls decayed quickly, to half its starting strength in 11.5 hours. The rapid decay of emanation and the contagion of its activity were also observed in Europe. A German chemist discovered radium emanation and Marie Curie detected the activity it induced.

The obvious next task was to learn the nature of emanation, its connection with thorium, and how it induced activity in other bodies. Rutherford rushed at the work. "My chief solace at present," he reassured Mary, "is to keep working." He had his eye not only on nature, but also on the Royal Society, to which he expected to be elected on the strength of his discoveries about radioactivity. "My dear girl [this was his most intimate endearment], I keep going steadily turning to the Lab. five nights out of seven, till 11 or 12 o'clock." Following this schedule, he stayed out of trouble and found that the emanation consisted of radioactive particles and that it, not the thorium directly, activated the walls of the tube.

With these puzzling results in hand, Rutherford at last broke off work, gave examinations to his students, and boarded the train to San Francisco to catch the steamer to New Zealand. The trip took a month. That gave him time to worry about his wedding. "I hope you are not figuring on a public wedding for me to make an ass of myself as all men do. I am not keen on these functions. However you have a free hand over my movements up to the wedding day and then your turn comes. . . . I do not belong to the henpecked variety of men so you must be prepared to be humble and meek. . . . Good bye my own love with as many kisses as is good for you." He did not have to worry—not about the wedding, anyway. Mary described it as "a very short and comparatively uninteresting affair." Only members of the two families, celebrating teetotally, were present. The return honeymoon through the United States and Canada was done in better style. The new couple entered Montreal with what remained of Rutherford's savings, around $1,000, and, what would prove much more valuable, a collection of puzzles about thorium.

A young scientist more confident even than Rutherford had appeared in Montreal just before the newlyweds arrived. This was Frederick Soddy, a chemist trained at Oxford. He had come all the way to Toronto in answer to

Frederick Soddy, Rutherford's collaborator in the discovery of radioactive disintegration, about 1905. Soddy never lost the unusual self-confidence that took him to Canada, helped him to identify the transmutation of atoms and, later, brought him to idiosyncratic notions about society, economics, and politics.

an advertisement of a job in the chemistry department of the university there without bothering to notify the department of his candidacy or to determine whether the position had been filled. It had, so Soddy went on to Montreal, to see the chemical sights. He liked them and accepted a junior position in the chemistry department at McGill.

Rutherford had asked the department's director to help him determine the nature of emanation. The director thought he had something better to do and threw away a chance at the Nobel prize. Soddy had nothing at all to do. He accepted Rutherford's invitation to seek the chemical nature of a ghost-like substance unavailable in weighable amounts and detectable only by its radioactivity, which disappeared in a few minutes. Thus began the partnership of Rutherford and Soddy, which transformed the field of radioactivity from random exploration into science. Despite the difficulties of their task, by January 1902, after a year of work, they had concentrated enough emanation to identify it as a gas belonging to the argon family.

This identification could not have been made much earlier. That is because no one knew of argon before 1894. Its detection belongs to a class of discoveries sharply different from those made by Roentgen and Becquerel. X rays and radioactivity were altogether new and surprising, unlike anything previously known. Argon offered no novelties to the physicist, though it presented a few curiosities to the chemist.

The argon story began when Lord Rayleigh, who had preceded Thomson as Cavendish professor, noticed that nitrogen derived from the air had an atomic weight slightly higher than that of nitrogen derived from chemical compounds. The obvious explanation, apart from error, was that the aerial nitrogen contained a heavier impurity, or the chemical nitrogen a lighter one. Rayleigh made the second choice. It was wrong. The correct answer, demonstrated by a professor of chemistry at the University of London, William Ramsay, is that air contains a small amount of an unusual gas that is heavier than nitrogen. This new gas declined to combine with any of the substances with which other gases delighted to unite. Rayleigh and Ramsay named it "argon" after a Greek word meaning "lazy" or "inert." During the next few years, while Rutherford began the study of radioactivity and Thomson discovered the corpuscle, Ramsay found a family of inert gases in the atmosphere. The lightest of them, helium, occurred not only in the air, but also in association with ores of uranium and thorium. Rutherford eventually demonstrated the nature and necessity of this association.

While Soddy determined that, chemically speaking, the emanation belonged among the inert gases, Rutherford studied the induced activity to which it gave rise. He tried exposing a negatively charged metal plate to the emanation; the plate became strongly radioactive. Evidently the emanation's activity was borne by a positively charged carrier. That agreed very well with Thomson's ideas of atomic structure, according to which the emission of a beta particle, or electron, would leave the atom with an excess positive charge. However, radioactivity seldom presents itself simply. The behavior of the induced activity on the negative plate depended on the length of time it remained in contact with the emanation. If the exposure were brief, the plate's activity rose; if long, its activity fell immediately after removal from contact with the emanation. The induction apparently took time.

It was time to make a picture. What was the relation of radioactivity—the emission of beta particles in this case—to the change of thorium into emanation and of emanation into the active deposit? Rutherford and Soddy devised the simple revolutionary answer—that the emission of a beta (or an alpha) particle *constitutes* radioactive change—after dissolving a complication that seemed to most researchers to plunge the subject into a deeper fog. The complication surfaced around 1900 when Becquerel managed to destroy the activity of a uranium salt by chemical treatment. When

Curves drawn by Rutherford in 1902 to show the rise and fall of activity of thorium and thorium X. The curve running from the upper left indicates the decay in the power of thorium X to produce emanation (100 is taken to be its power immediately after separation from its parent thorium). The curve rising from the lower left indicates the recovery of the emanating power of the thorium after removal of its X component. In just over four days ThX has lost half of its activity and Th has regained half.

he examined the salt a few months later, however, he found that it had regained its power. He doubted that he had observed correctly and asked William Crookes, an English chemist who had toyed with radioactivity, to check his results. Crookes succeeded immediately in making all his uranium salts duds by extracting from each a radioactive product differing in chemical properties from uranium. He labelled this radiator "uranium X," which nicely expressed almost everything he knew about it. Unlike uranium, uranium X emitted only beta particles and gradually lost its intensity. While it died off, however, the uranium salts from which it came again became radioactive. The death of the extract seemed to revive its source.

A week before Christmas 1901 Crookes reported these strange facts to McGill. Rutherford and Soddy tried the same operation on thorium, which they divided into an

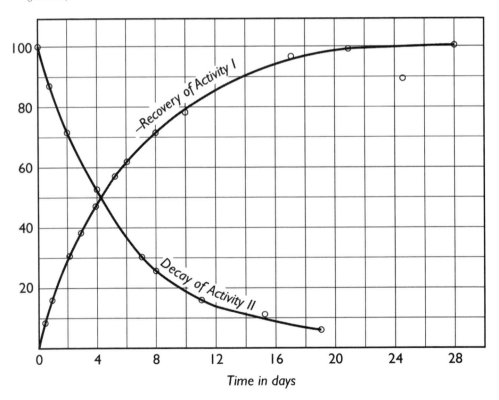

inert thorium and a beta-emitting thorium X; in four days thorium X had lost half its strength and the inert thorium had regained half its initial power. Rutherford and Soddy showed this behavior in two dramatic curves indicating the intensities of the recovering thorium and the declining thorium X. Rutherford later put these curves in the center of his baronial shield. What had happened to the thorium X? And what had it to do with the emanation?

By mid-1902, Rutherford and Soddy could say that thorium X (ThX) arises from thorium (Th), and the emanation (Em) from ThX, by "subatomic chemical change" (presumably a rearrangement of corpuscles preceding alpha or beta emission) indicated by radioactivity. By the end of the year they could be bolder and clearer: an atom of thori-

In this summary of knowledge about radioactive decay drawn up in 1904, "α Pt" signifies alpha particle; "β Pt," beta particle (electron); and "γ Ray," gamma ray, a high-energy X ray. The decay series beginning with uranium includes the sequence starting with radium. Radium's parent, ionium, identified in 1907, is three generations removed from Uranium X.

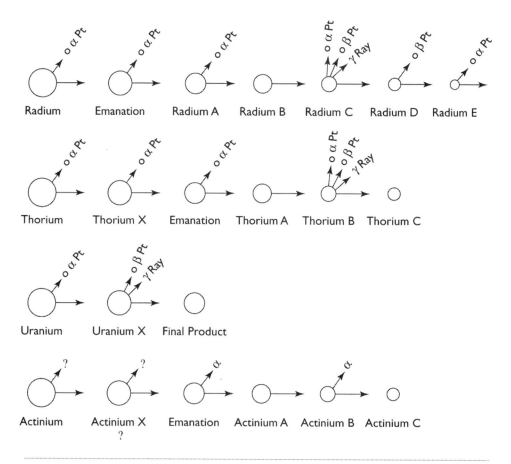

41

um or uranium (U) *becomes* an atom of ThX or UX *as* it emits an alpha ray, and an atom of ThX or UX becomes one of ThEm or UEm while emitting a beta ray. Similarly, the emanations throw off active deposits that continue the process of natural radioactive decay. Where did it all end? Was the world disintegrating? Did the presence of helium in uranium and thorium ores signify that ultimately the earth would transmute itself into an inert gas? This alarming scenario did not worry Rutherford and Soddy. By the time they announced their theory, they knew, though they could not prove, that helium is a byproduct, not the endpoint, of radioactive decay.

Their main evidence was an experiment of Rutherford's that materialized the alpha ray. Previous attempts by Rutherford and others to bend alpha rays electrically or magnetically had failed. That was the main evidence for regarding them as immaterial agents like X rays. Rutherford finally succeeded in bending the paths of alpha particles by applying a very strong electric field to the radiation from a good bit of radium, some 19,000 times as strong as uranium, which Marie Curie had given him. In his enthusiasm over this feat, Rutherford inadvertently grounded his apparatus through himself and received a great shock. Soddy was there. "I recall seeing him dancing like a dervish and emitting extraordinary imprecations, probably in the Maori tongue." The painful materialization of the alpha ray fit it into Thomson's picture of the atom and the Rutherford-Soddy theory of radioactive decay: In alpha emission, as in beta emission, an atom throws off a piece of itself in the process of changing chemical species.

The materialization of the alpha particle made alpha emission a more weighty support for the theory of spontaneous chemical change than the beta emissions from which Rutherford and Soddy inferred it. The reason lies at the heart of atomic theory. The beta particle is an electron. The removal of an electron from an atom constitutes ionization,

text continues on page 45

The identifying mark of a charged particle, its *e/m*, indicates the ratio of the strength with which an electric or magnetic force acts on it to the inertia with which it resists changing its direction. To bend an alpha ray, with its relatively large mass, requires a much stronger force than a similar exercise on a beta ray. Rutherford succeeded in bending alpha rays when Marie Curie's radium gave him a source intense enough to enable him to use an electric force of

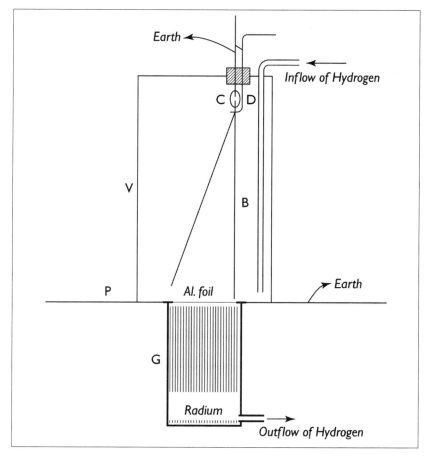

The apparatus with which Rutherford demonstrated that alpha rays are streams of material particles.

continued on page 44

continued from page 43

attainable strength. The connection between the intensity of the source and the strength of the field appears from the figure, which illustrates the typically simple apparatus Rutherford employed.

The radium placed at the bottom of the lower chamber sent its rays through the parallel plates G into the electroscope V, where they ionized the air and caused the charged leaves of the detector to collapse. (This is the fundamental effect discovered by Rutherford and Thomson in their experiment on ionization by X rays.) The hydrogen flow indicated on the diagram drove back the emanation to keep it and its products from contaminating the experiment.

If an electric force powerful enough to drive some of the alpha particles into the plates could be obtained, the ionization in the chamber V would fall and the rate of discharge of the leaves would diminish. The closer the plates, the stronger the field that can be developed between them. But the narrower their separation, the fewer the rays that can get all the way to V, since only those fired very close to the vertical would avoid hitting the plates even in the absence of an electric field. The greater the number of particles emitted, the narrower the gap that a detectable number can traverse. That is why Rutherford needed an intense source. The same argument applies to a magnetic field. By measuring the values of the fields when the rate of collapse of the electroscope reached a minimum, Rutherford could calculate the e/m of the alpha particle in the same way that Thomson had found that of the corpuscle.

text continued from page 42

which changes the atom's physical properties but not its chemical nature. How, in Thomson's model of the atom, does beta emission, which also involves the loss of an electron, differ from ionization? Soddy, who had not been through Cambridge, probably saw more quickly than Rutherford the profound difference between radioactive decay and ordinary physical and chemical processes like ionization. But when Rutherford could grasp the alpha particle electrically and magnetically, and so could determine its charge-to-mass ratio, he knew immediately that alpha emission had to result in a change of chemical species. That was because the measured ratio implied that the alpha particle had a mass at least twice that of hydrogen.

According to the periodic table of the elements, the weight of an atom determines its chemical properties. The difference of only one unit of weight, the weight of a hydrogen atom, was, and is, dramatic: argon, weighing in at 40, is a chemically inert gas; potassium, at 39, is a very reactive metal. Rutherford and his school eventually remodeled and reinterpreted the periodic table; Soddy would win a Nobel prize for his part in the affair. In 1902, however, the relation between atomic weight and chemical properties expressed in the table of elements required that in losing the weight of an alpha particle, an atom would necessarily change species, that is, one element would become another.

If an alpha particle weighed something more than a hydrogen atom, it should be the ion of some known or unknown light element. The identification was not far to seek. The occurrence of helium in uranium and thorium ores pointed the way. Rutherford and Soddy conjectured that the alpha particle was nothing but a helium atom minus two electrons. (Since the mass of helium was known to be around four times hydrogen's, the arithmetic worked out if the alpha particle had twice the charge on the hydrogen ion.) It took Rutherford several years to confirm that conjecture.

text continues on page 50

	I.	II.	III.	IV.	V.	VI.	VII.	VIII.
				RH_4	RH_3	RH_2	RH	
Series	R_2O	RO	R_2O_3	RO_2	R_2O_5	RO_3	R_2O_7	RO_4
1 2	H = 1 Li 7	Be 9.4	B 11	C 12	N 14	O 16	F 19	
3	Na 23	Mg 24	Al 27.3	Si 28	P 31	S 32	Cl 35.5	
4	K 39	Ca 40	— 44	Ti 48	V 51	Cr 52	Mn 55	Fe 56 Co 59 Ni 59 Cu 63
5	(Cu 63)	Zn 65	— 68	— 72	As 75	Se 78	Br 80	
6	Rb 85	Sr 87	(?) Yt 88	Zr 90	Nb 94	Mo 96	— 100	Ru 104 Rh 1 Pd 106 Ag ?
7	Ag (108)	Cd 112	In 113	Sn 118	Sb 122	Te 125	I 127	
8	Cs 133	Ba 137	(?) Di 138	(?) Ce 140	—	—	—	
9	(—)	----	—	—	—	—	—	
10	—	—	(?) Er 178	(?) La 180	Ta 182	W 184	—	Os 195 Ir I Pt 198 Au
11	(Au 199)	Hg 200	Tl 204	Pb 207	Bi 208	—	—	
12	—	—	—	Th 231	—	U 240	—	

The definitive form of Mendeleev's table of the elements (1871).

J ust before the discovery of the argon family, chemists recognized some 73 elements, or substances that they could not decompose into simpler ones. The smallest bit of matter possessing the chemical properties of an element was its atom. There is a vast number of these atoms in even the smallest visible object, over a billion billion of them, for example, in the ink in the period at the end of this sentence. The chemists of 1900 believed that every atom of a given element had the same weight, unique to that element, which could therefore be identified fully by the weight of one of its atoms. Since a billion billion atoms fit into a period, the weight of each is vanishingly small. The lightest atom, that of hydrogen gas, weighs just over a billionth of a billionth of a billionth of a kilogram; the heaviest atom known in 1900, uranium, weighs around 238 times as much. In order to avoid having to deal with awkward numbers, and also because, in 1900, they did not know the absolute weights of the atoms very precisely, chemists and physicists gave atomic weights in multiples of that of hydrogen, which is taken as one. Thus the "weight"—that is, the weight relative to hydrogen—of helium, the second lightest element, is 4; of nitrogen, 14; of argon, 40; and, as we know, of uranium, 238.

These round numbers suggested that the weights of all the atoms were integral (whole-number) multiples of hydrogen's; but some atomic weights, notoriously chlorine's at 35.45, copper's at 63.54, and mercury's at 200.59, robustly refused to come out integral no matter how hard chemists labored to purify them. The question of what determined the weights and how the weights determined chemical properties intrigued physical scientists for over a century before progress in radioactivity provided definite answers.

Since the elements can be characterized by a number—the weight of their atoms—they can be ordered. It would not have been of much interest to list them in a single column according to weight. However, when displayed in a two-dimensional format according to the rule that elements with similar chemical properties stand in the same columns and elements close in atomic weight follow one another in the same rows, the apparently arbitrary classification by numbers became a conjuror's trick with extraordinary and mysterious power.

THE PERIODIC TABLE OF THE ELEMENTS

Groups.	0	I.	II.	III.	IV.	V.	VI.	VII.	VIII.		
Series.	...	...	...	...	RH_4	RH_3	RH_2	RH_1	...		
	...	R_2O	R_2O_2	R_2O_3	R_2O_4	R_2O_5	R_2O_6	R_2O_7	R_2O_8		
1		H 1.008									
2	He 4	Li 7	Be 9.1	B 11	C 12	N 14.01	O 16	F 19			
3	Ne 20	Na 23	Mg 24.32	Al 27.1	Si 28.3	P 31	S 32.07	Cl 35.46			
4	A 39.9	K 39.1	Ca 40.09	Sc 44.1	Ti 48.1	V 51.2	Cr 52.1	Mn 54.93	Fe 55.85	Co 58.97	Ni ?
5	—	Cu 63.57	Zn 65.37	Ga 69.9	Ge 72.5	As 75	Se 79.2	Br 79.92			
6	Kr 81.8	Rb 85.45	Sr 87.62	Y 89	Zr 90.6	Cb (Nb) 93.5	Mo 96	—	Ru 101.7	Rh 103	Pd
7	—	Ag 107.88	Cd 112.4	In 114.8	Sn 119	Sb 120.2	Te 127.5	I 126.92			
8	Xe 128	Cs 132.81	Ba 137.37	La 139	Ce 140.25	—	—	—			
9	—	—				—	—	—	—		
10	—	—	—	—	—	Ta 181	W 184	—	Os 190.9	Ir 193.1	Pt
11	—	Au 197.2	Hg 200	Tl 204.1	Pb 207.1	Bi 208	—	—			
12	—	—	Ra 226.4	—	Th 232.42	—	U 238.5	—			

The periodic table in 1909.

The table is called "periodic" because similar elements recur or repeat after a certain number of horizontal spaces. The preceding figure shows a piece of one of the first tables drawn up by the inventor of this mode of display, the Russian chemist Dmitri Mendeleev. When his two rules conflicted—when strict ordering by weight in the rows brought elements into the wrong columns (the wrong chemical families)—he left spaces. He guessed, correctly, that nature held undiscovered elements that would fill the spaces and he estimated their atomic weights and chemical properties from the positions of the holes that were to receive them. When alerted where to look, chemists quickly found the missing elements between calcium and titanium, and below aluminum and silicon. The new elements received the names scandium, gallium, and germanium after the native countries of their discoverers (Sweden, France, and Germany), thus establishing a practice that Marie Curie was to invoke in calling her first discovery polonium.

The radioelements identified before 1900 fit into the table of the elements. Thorium (atomic weight, A, of 232) and uranium already had places. Radium ($A = 226$) and polonium ($A = 210$) fit into unoccupied spaces above barium in the family of alkali earths, and between bismuth ($A = 209$) and thorium, respectively. Astonishingly, the argon family—no member of which was known when Mendeleev drew up his table—found a place at the table, or almost. Chemists opened a new column, with helium ($A = 4$) at its head and radium emanation ($A = 222$) at its bottom. The only point of pressure was the pater familias, argon ($A = 40$), which was overweight; according to its chemical properties, it had to come before potassium ($A = 39$), which, by the rules of the table, it should have followed. This problem, and similar inversions of cobalt and nickel and tellurium and iodine, were also cleared up through the study of radioactivity.

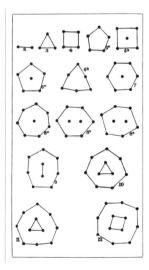
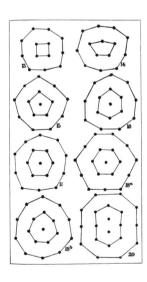

J. J. Thomson's analogy between floating magnets in a magnetic field and the arrangement of electrons in an atom (p. 29) provided a rough explanation of the periodic properties of the elements. The floating magnetic needles distribute themselves into concentric circles as their number increases. The figure was made by laying sheets of paper on the inked tips of the needles.

text continued from page 45

The collaboration with Soddy and the work on alpha particles left a great vacuum in the new science of radioactivity. It lacked a textbook. Rutherford hurried to provide one. His book first appeared in 1904, had a second edition the following year, and a third, translated into German, in 1913. It defined and dominated the subject for a generation. The writing, which would have been a full-time job for most men, did not keep Rutherford from research, teaching, and lecturing in Canada, the United States, and England.

He lectured in London in 1904. The venerable Lord Kelvin, then 80, was one of his most attentive listeners. In one of his talks, Rutherford touched on the age of the earth, a question that Kelvin had investigated in order to combat the theory of evolution. According to Kelvin's calculations, if the earth and sun had been cooling at their present rate for as long as Darwin required to transmute an amoeba into a man, the solar system long since would have grown too cold to support life. Rutherford and Soddy's disintegration theory undercut Kelvin's argument in two ways: the process of radioactive decay provided a source of heat that Kelvin had ignored, and the rate of decay showed the earth to be far older than he had allowed.

A confrontation appeared inevitable. Rutherford often described it. "I came into the [lecture] room, which was half dark, and presently spotted Lord Kelvin. . . . To my relief, he fell asleep, but as I came to the important point, I saw the old bird sit up, open an eye, and cock a baleful glance at me. Then a sudden inspiration came, and I said Lord Kelvin had limited the age of the earth, *provided no new source* [of heat] *was discovered*. That prophetic utterance refers to what we are now considering tonight, radium! Behold! The old boy beamed upon me."

During his years at McGill Rutherford labored as a man possessed. "I have to publish my present work as rapidly as possible in order to keep in the race," he wrote his mother in January 1902. "The best sprinters in this road of investigation are Becquerel and the Curies in Paris." In 1903 the French sprinters shared the third Nobel prize for physics. The previous winners have already appeared in our story: Roentgen, the first-ever Nobel prize–winner in physics, in 1901, and Lorentz and Zeeman, the winners for 1902. The award to the French pushed Rutherford to redouble his efforts to outdo them. The physics prize for 1904 went to Rayleigh for his part in the discovery of argon (Ramsay got the chemistry prize). At this news, Rutherford, who had just received a gold medal from the Royal Society, wrote Mary, then on a visit home, "I may have a chance [at the Nobel prize] if I keep going, in another ten years or so, as there are a good many prominent physicists like J. J. and others to have their turn spending the money."

J. J. had his turn in 1906. Expectation mounted while several universities in the United States tried to capture the star who had outshone their best physicists. Rutherford refused all offers, since none came with enough money to sway him or held the promise of laboratory facilities better than his own. Not that everything was to his liking at McGill. He never succeeded in setting up a research school there to compete with Thomson's at the Cavendish. Although the physics department taught many undergraduates, very few continued for advanced training. Rutherford raised some undergraduates to research assistants, notably Harriet Brooks, who worked with him on a determination, which was not very exact, of the atomic weight of radium emanation. After graduation, she received a fellowship with Thomson in Cambridge.

For a time, before his methods became widely known through his textbooks and Soddy's lectures in England (Soddy left McGill in 1902 to work with Ramsay in London), advanced students came from the United States and central Europe to learn at the source. The traffic was uncertain, however, and brought only half a dozen people into the laboratory during Rutherford's tenure. The first

Rutherford's graduate student Harriet Brooks stands with her colleagues in this photo taken around 1899 (Rutherford is on the far right). Brookes was the first woman to earn an MA at McGill University.

was a woman, Fanny Cook Gates, the head of the physics department at Goucher College in Baltimore. The most successful, who arrived in Montreal in 1905, was the chemist Otto Hahn, who became a power in German science and a Nobel prize–winner for his part in the discovery of atomic fission, the splitting of atomic nuclei utilized in nuclear weapons and atomic energy.

Hahn had been studying with Ramsay to perfect his English and his education. While in London he complicated the sequence of transformations given by Rutherford and Soddy by discovering an alpha–emitting product between

Th and ThX, which he called radiothorium (RaTh). Thorium X remained the immediate parent of ThEm but was no longer, as Rutherford and Soddy had taught, the direct descendant of thorium. This news did not delight Rutherford's camp. "[Hahn's element] is only a new compound of thorium X and stupidity." These words come from a letter to Rutherford from his outspoken friend at Yale, the radiochemist Bertrand Boltwood. Rutherford accepted this unfriendly evaluation. He did not have a high opinion of work done in Ramsay's lab. "I think he [Hahn] will 'take *physic* and *throw up* his element.'" This dainty reply to Boltwood referred to Hahn's impending arrival in Montreal, where he would be given physics to cure him of his chemical errors. Hahn nonetheless made good his claim and, after returning to Germany, muddied the water further by finding two more radioactive substances, which he called mesothoriums, both beta emitters, in the decay sequence between Th and RaTh.

Hahn was not the only chemist who complicated the Rutherford–Soddy series. It turned out that two or more radioproducts stood between uranium and uranium X. That made the relationship between uranium and radium even more perplexing. A vigorous search for radium's immediate parent ensued; Boltwood found it, and baptized it ionium, in 1907. A third radioactive series, descended from "actinium," a substance discovered in 1899 by a colleague of the Curies', further increased the number of known naturally radioactive materials, as did exploration of the active deposits of the emanations descended from all three ancestors uranium, thorium, and actinium. By 1907, when Rutherford at last left McGill, some 26 radioactive substances, differing in their lifetimes, emissions, and chemical properties, had been identified. This was too much of a good thing. What determined the sequence of decay? How did all those radioactive substances relate to the periodic table of the elements?

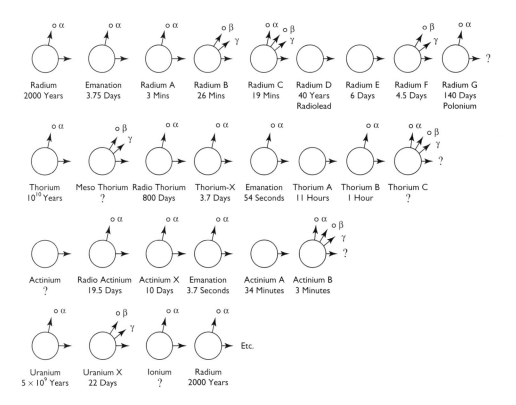

The increase of knowledge about natural radioactive decay since 1904 (see page 41) includes the placement of radium and its products in the uranium series and an indication of the "half-life"—the time in which a radio-element loses half of its activity—of most of the products. The half-life of ThX given here as 3.7 days improved on the value of just over four days found by Rutherford and Soddy in 1902.

The answer that Rutherford and Soddy gave was that each radioactive species was a new, distinctive element. That seemed obvious. Uranium and thorium already had places in the periodic table when their radioactivity was detected. Radium turned out to be a heavier version of barium and went into an unoccupied space at the top of the table's column of alkali earths. Similarly, polonium and actinium fit easily into the table above their chemical cousins tellurium and lanthanum; and the emanations belonged to the family of inert gases.

But there came the trouble. Were there really three chemically different inert radioactive gases? If so, how could the periodic system accommodate them? Since their ancestors uranium, thorium, and actinium necessarily had different atomic weights, so, probably, did they; and yet it appeared that they had very similar if not identical chemical properties. How could they be put into the table in accordance with the rules that elements with different atomic weights have different chemical properties and that when arranged in order of weights, the elements fall into distinct families with similar chemical properties?

As the periodic table began to suffer the pressures of overpopulation, Rutherford received a job offer he could not refuse. The physics institute at the University of Manchester, England, had furnishings and equipment similar to those in MacDonald's building at McGill. It had a larger staff and more research students, and its own endowed fellowship, the John Harling, which its director could award as he pleased. The director, Arthur Schuster, a completely anglicized German, had played a part in the deciphering of cathode rays. He wanted to retire, but would do so only if the university would appoint Rutherford in his place. Rutherford jumped at the chance to head an up-to-date laboratory in the middle of England. He accepted and offered the John Harling fellowship to Harriet Brooks. She accepted but then resigned it in favor of marriage. Even Rutherford did not win them all.

Hans Geiger (left) and Rutherford in Montreal around 1912.

Manchester and the Structure of Atoms

Rutherford arrived in Manchester in the fall of 1907. His laboratory was the only thing that interested him in the city, which, despite its grime, had an excellent symphony orchestra and a lively theater. The laboratory almost fully met his expectations. He had a good mechanic and glassblower, excellent equipment, and a cooperative staff. He wrote A. S. Eve, a close colleague from Canada: "Everybody seems jolly & anxious to help and I find a most enjoyable absence of convention." The students pleased him too. He wrote Boltwood: "I find the students here regard a full professor as little short of Lord God Almighty. It is quite refreshing after the critical attitude of Canadian students." The only fly in his Eden was the lab's lack of radioactive material.

Rutherford soon had a good supply of the most costly radiator of all, radium, thanks to the generosity of colleagues in Vienna. Bohemia, then part of the Austro-Hungarian Empire, possessed rich deposits of uranium ores, and the Radium Institute of the Austrian Academy of Sciences had more radium than it could use. The Academy agreed to loan Rutherford radium for his research on the nature of alpha particles. The loan came with a string

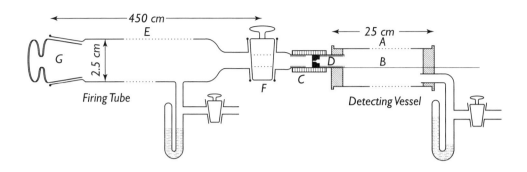

The experimental arrangement with which Geiger and Rutherford started to count alpha particles in 1908. The radioactive source (not shown) sat in a hollow iron cylinder that could be moved by a magnet from outside the firing tube (E). When the stopcock at F was opened, three to five alphas a minute squeezed through the narrow opening at C and a thin window of mica at D to ionize the gas in the detecting vessel (A). The wire (B) collects the ions. The vertical piping below indicates the pumping system for making partial vacuums in E and A.

attached, however: it had to be shared with Ramsay, to whom it was delivered. Ramsay proposed to keep it all for a year or more and, in compensation, to send Rutherford every week by courier whatever emanation the Viennese sample and his own stock of radium produced. Rutherford protested, Ramsay insisted, and radiological warfare was averted only by a timely gift by the Viennese to Rutherford of another sample for his own use. The alpha rays from Vienna were to make history in Manchester.

Ever since his rough measurement of the charge-to-mass ratio of the alpha particle in 1902, Rutherford had looked for ways to improve his numbers and define the nature of the particle. His earliest result made its $e/m = 6,000$ on a scale on which the hydrogen ion's $e/m = 9,650$. On the assumption that the alpha particle and the ion carried the same charge, the alpha's mass would be 1.6 times hydrogen's, or, in Rutherford's easygoing way, nearly twice. If, however, the alpha particle had double the charge of the hydrogen ion, its mass would be over three times hydrogen's, or, again in Rutherfordian approximation, four times. But the mass of helium is about four times hydrogen's. That was enough for Rutherford to claim that an alpha and a doubly ionized helium ion (a helium atom that had lost two electrons) were one and the same.

Rutherford's thinking was open to the objection that it assumed that all alpha particles were intrinsically the same, an assumption for which no good evidence existed. To remove the objection Rutherford examined the alpha rays from many different radioactive substances and always obtained roughly the same value for their e/m. This value came out smaller than the original one, around 5,070 as against hydrogen's 9,650, which supported Rutherford's conjecture that helium's e/m was one-half hydrogen's. He had proceeded this far before he left Canada. In Manchester he had the combination that enabled him to resolve all doubts: Hans Geiger from Erlangen and radium from Vienna. Geiger had come to Manchester from Germany in 1906 as Schuster's assistant; Rutherford persuaded him to stay on and help track the alpha particle. Together they invented a tube that could count each alpha particle fired into it separately. Later, perfected and miniaturized, it became that indispensable tool of nuclear physics, the Geiger counter.

In its early version the counter consisted of two partially evacuated glass tubes connected by a fitting with a tiny hole in its center. One tube contained the alpha-emitting source on a small glass vessel with walls thick enough to retain the source but thin enough to pass alpha particles. The second tube contained a dilute gas under an electric field, as in the apparatus with which Rutherford had discovered alpha and beta rays. The length of the firing tube and the size of the hole ensured that only one alpha particle at a time entered the counting chamber. When it did, it ionized the gas and a current passed to a wire running down the axis of the tube.

Knowing by this method how many alpha particles the source shot into the counter in an hour, say, Rutherford and Geiger could figure out the total number N emitted in the same time in all directions; that was only geometry. To find the charge carried by a single alpha particle, they had only to catch all N particles on a conductor connected to a current meter. The meter gave the total charge Q carried by the N particles. Anyone could then deduce the charge on a single alpha particle: it was Q/N, which, with the

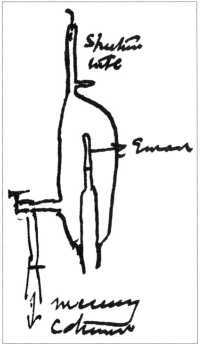

The apparatus that Rutherford and Thomas Royds used in 1908 to show that alpha particles are helium nuclei appears on the right. The figure on the left is Rutherford's sketch from which the glass blower made the upper part of the apparatus.

experimental numbers obtained by Rutherford and Geiger, worked out to something more than twice the charge on the electron as determined at the Cavendish. According to Rutherford's earlier result, the alpha particle's e/m was half that of hydrogen's. It followed from this value and Rutherford and Geiger's measurement of Q/N that the weight of an alpha particle was 4, just the weight of helium.

The weakness of this identification was that it depended on a value for e about 150% higher than the Cavendish's best number. To secure his value for the electronic charge and his identification of alpha particles with helium nuclei, Rutherford and a research student drew off radium emanation into a glass tube thin enough that the alpha particles emitted by the confined emanation could penetrate its walls. They sealed this tube inside a vessel entirely free from helium and pumped out the air it contained. As the emanation died away in the thin inner tube, alpha particles crossed into the evacuated vessel, picked up stray electrons there, and became helium atoms. When enough were present, Rutherford sent an electric spark through the vessel and saw the spectrum of helium where no helium had been before. This beautiful and characteristically simple experiment was performed in 1908. It came at a good time. For in that year Rutherford got his Nobel prize. At his obligatory lecture in Stockholm, he reviewed his work on the nature of the rays from radioactive substances and ended with his dramatic observation of the spectrum of helium grown from alpha particles.

Rutherford had expected to receive the physics prize after J. J. Thomson had been honored. He misguessed. He received the prize for chemistry, he for whom "damn fool" and "chemist" were almost synonyms. His transformation from a physicist was one of the fastest and most puzzling "disintegrations" he had ever witnessed. He said so at the Nobel banquet in Stockholm. His Swedish hosts were amused. They knew how the transformation had happened.

Rutherford had bolstered the case for his high value of e (as against the smaller number measured at the Cavendish) by observing that Max Planck had obtained the same large value from his theory of radiation. The Swedish Nobel committees for chemistry and physics admired exact measurements. They agreed that Planck would receive the prize for physics and Rutherford the prize for chemistry in the same year. In this way Rutherford and Geiger's counting of individual ions, confirmed by Planck's theory of radiation, would offer compelling proof of the modern theory of matter. The proposal was defeated by the Swedish Academy of Sciences, which doubted Planck's theory and had the final say on the choice of laureates. The decision left Rutherford in chemistry without a suitable partner in physics.

En route to Stockholm, where, as Rutherford reported to Eve, he and Mary had the time of their lives, he attended a banquet given in his honor by Thomson at the Cavendish. One of the physicists contributed a hymn to

Rutherford's main collaborator in his prize-winning work. It ran in part like this:

An alpha ray was I, contented with my lot
From Radium C I was set free
And outwards I was shot . . .
And on my wild career, as swiftly on I flew,
A rarefied gas wouldn't let me pass
But I shoved my way quite through.
I had some lively tussles
To make it ionize
But I set the small corpuscles
Abuzzing 'round like flies . . .
I murmured "Botheration!"
(A word that's most obscene)
And I made a scintillation
As I struck a zinc-blende screen . . .
But now I'm settled down and I move about quite slow,
For I, alas, am helium gas
Since I got that dreadful blow.

The Rutherfords in the car they bought with the prize money Rutherford received as the winner of the Nobel Prize in Chemistry for 1908.

text continues on page 64

HELIUM FROM ALPHA PARTICLES

When a gas is made to conduct electricity, as in neon tubes or sodium lamps, the gas glows in a manner characteristic of the atoms of which it is composed. When viewed through a prism, this glow breaks down into a series of bright lines of sharp, discontinuous colors collectively called a spectrum; the spectrum of an atom is as good an indicator, indeed, a better indicator, of its nature than its atomic weight. Physicists supposed that electrons moving inside atoms gave rise to spectrum lines. Since, in 1908, Rutherford thought that alpha particles contained electrons, he had to suppose that they had a spectrum; but since no one had ever seen it, he had also to suppose that it did not consist of visible light. In contrast, helium had a beautiful spectrum, well known and easily observed. When, therefore, he started with a vessel free from helium into which he fired alpha particles and saw the spectrum of helium gradually appear and intensify as the experiment continued, he inferred that the particles had collected the electrons they needed to produce visible spectral lines. Since an alpha particle plus electrons appeared to be a helium atom, it followed that the atom minus the electrons was the alpha particle.

text continued from page 62

The return journey from Stockholm, through Germany to Holland and across the Channel to England, was also a triumph. Hahn organized trips to all the main physics laboratories in Berlin, and all the Berlin physicists attended a farewell banquet for the new laureate in chemistry. In Leyden Rutherford visited Lorentz, whose work had been key in promoting Thomson's corpuscle into a general constituent of atoms. Travel occasioned by the Nobel award did not end with the Rutherfords' return to Cambridge. He used his prize money to buy an automobile, which the lab mechanic kept running. Rutherford liked to travel. He went on motoring excursions in England and in Europe, where he met with his former students, and he made long journeys by ship to the United States, Canada, Australia, New Zealand, and South Africa. Although he worked very hard, he always took a vacation, sometimes twice a year and frequently at the seaside, in cold England or on the warm Riviera.

Rutherford and Geiger had trouble getting their counter to work reliably. Every alpha particle did not generate the same number of ions as it passed down the counting tube. Since the discrepancy was great enough to menace the fundamental assumption that only one particle entered the counter at a time, it had to be explored and explained. After much fiddling, they traced the differences in ionization current to the deflection of alpha particles by collisions with the apparatus or with molecules of the residual gas. Deflected particles had shorter or longer paths through the counter than ones that went straight down the axis; the path length determined the amount of ionization produced and hence the current collected on the plates.

To achieve greater uniformity in the paths, Rutherford and Geiger lengthened the counting tube; they stopped with an apparatus almost 5 meters (15 feet) long, which behaved well enough for their purposes. They could hardly quit there. Rutherford had become used to picturing the alpha particle as a structure the size of an atom—not a flimsy thing like an electron, which could be knocked about by any electromagnetic breeze, but a vigorous, powerful customer, a Rutherford of radiations. It surprised him that collisions could knock an alpha particle off course enough to affect its ionization trail appreciably. He asked Geiger to find out just how far an atom could push aside a thundering alpha particle.

Geiger modified their apparatus to suit by placing a thin metal foil in the path of the particles and replacing the counter by a sheet of fluorescent material that gave off a tiny flash of light whenever a particle struck it. He examined these flashes through a microscope in a dark room. When he removed the foil, the flashes all occurred close to the axis of the tube. With an aluminum foil in place, the area that showed flashes enlarged; with a gold foil it expanded still further and a few alpha particles turned through an appreciable angle struck the screen far outside the area originally affected. Indeed, Geiger could not find a limit. Rutherford suggested looking for alphas rebounding from the gold foil back toward the source. A research student, Ernest Marsden, later John Harling Fellow and Geiger's successor as Rutherford's assistant, and ultimately a professor of physics in New Zealand, joined in the experiment. They found the ricocheting particles immediately.

The success amazed Rutherford. He like to recall it as the most "incredible event" he had ever witnessed, odder even than the suicide of atoms, as bizarre, he would say, as a cannonball bouncing off a piece of tissue paper. For where in the atom could there be a seat of force strong enough to turn around a heavy charged particle plowing ahead at an appreciable fraction of the speed of light? In solving this puzzle, which originated as a technical difficulty in a measuring instrument, Rutherford demonstrated the power of both British pictorial physics and his own vivid imagination, set the basis for the modern theory of the atom, and presided over a research group even stronger than the one Thomson had assembled to exploit the discovery of X rays.

The observation of the reflection of alpha particles from very thin metal foils had such grand consequences because of the stage to which Thomson had by then (1909) carried his model of the atom. In his original conception, in which the entire weight of the atom was contributed by its corpuscles, even the lightest atom, hydrogen, had more than a thousand constituents. To look more deeply, Thomson invented the technique of studying the transmission of the newly discovered rays through metal foils.

A beam of X or cathode rays will spread beyond its original limits owing to collisions with corpuscles in the foil's atoms. Thomson made the reasonable assumption that the spreading is proportional to the number of corpuscles present. But experiment showed that with this assumption there could be nowhere near 200,000 corpuscles in an atom of gold. (Since the atomic weight of gold is 197, it would have around 200,000 corpuscles if hydrogen had 1,000.) How many corpuscles did gold and other heavy elements have? Thomson phrased his answers as a ratio between A, the atomic weight of an element, and n, the number of its corpuscles. By 1906 he had worked n/A down from 1,000 to around 2. That brought two important consequences. One was that the positive part of the atom, which was needed to hold the corpuscles together, carried most of the atomic weight. The other was that if the ratio $n/A = 2$ also held for light elements like hydrogen and helium, Thomson's model atoms would have to struggle for survival.

According to the laws of electromagnetism, charged particles moving in circles must radiate energy. The electrons (corpuscles) in Thomson's model atoms thus faced the danger of radiating away all their energy of motion and falling down dead to the center of the atom. They also faced the danger of being knocked out of their orbits by repulsive forces from the other electrons in the atom. Thomson showed that when the rings contained many electrons the catastrophe could be averted. But this solution was

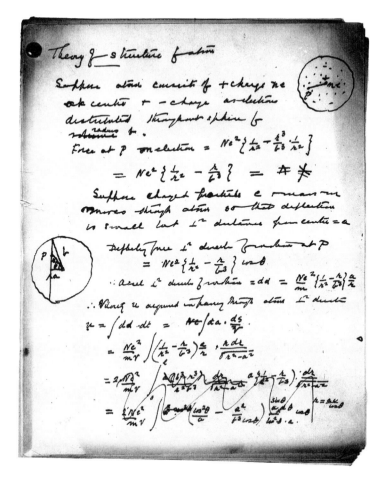

Rutherford's first sketch of his theory of the nuclear atom made in 1910. The upper drawing shows the atomic electrons around a small positive scattering center or nucleus marked +ne; the lower drawing shows the path of the alpha ray (the vertical line) through the atom. The inclusion of the electrons, a relic of Thomson's understanding of the scattering process, misled Rutherford into the unnecessary calculations crossed out at the bottom of the page.

not available for the light elements, especially hydrogen, which, if his rule n/A held, had only two electrons.

Since, in Thomson's picture, the alpha particle should have six electrons (8 from the rule $n = 2A$ less 2 from ionization), its passage through metal atoms would involve interactions between several pairs of particles. The collision process might be likened to the interpenetration of two meteor swarms. What then turned Rutherford's alpha particles around? The collision of an alpha particle's electron with an electron in the target atom might be a serious matter to the electrons, but not for the alpha or the atom. Rutherford reasoned that the only way a collision could be so effective as to cause the alpha particle to rebound as a whole would be to have all the positive charges of the atom collected at a point. They would then all act together on a foreign charged particle. The circulating electrons have very little effect on an alpha particle passing by them; the concentrated positive charge—Rutherford called it the atomic nucleus—has the power to bend the alpha particle's track in the manner observed by Geiger and Marsden.

Where was this hypothetical center and how big was it? To locate it by shooting alpha particles—structures Rutherford then imagined to be as large as atoms—at metal foils would be like looking for a safe by firing rockets through a bank. He thought again and again about the alphas' meeting with the scattering centers, putting himself in their places, calculating the pushes and deflections. Gradually and probably unconsciously, he came to picture the heavy alpha particle not as an atomic ion, but as a point. A helium atom minus two electrons would therefore be a body very small in comparison with an atom. It would have no electrons. It would be a bare nucleus, virtually a point, with a positive charge of two.

For the point alpha particle, the ratio n/A was not 2, as Thomson's rule predicted, but $\frac{1}{2}$. What about gold? Here Thomson's rule, which required $n = 400$, gave too great a push between the target nuclei and the point alpha particle. But a nuclear charge of 100 accounted for the phenomena perfectly. Hence, following Rutherford's thinking, at both the heavy and the light end of the table of elements the number of electrons in an atom equaled about half its atomic weight. That was very gratifying. Still, there were many difficulties—for example, how the hundred charges stayed together in the gold nucleus. The problem was all the more intriguing because the gold nucleus, though 50 times as heavy as an alpha particle, did not appear to take up any more space. For purposes of collision theory at least, a gold nucleus is no bigger than an alpha particle which is no bigger than an electron. Size is not a reliable indicator of weight.

As a model of the collision of alpha particles with matter, nothing could have been finer than Rutherford's nuclear atom. But the model suffered more gravely than Thomson's from instability. To explain the origin of the characteristic line spectra of the elements and other phenomena not connected with radioactivity and collisions, it seemed necessary to hold to Thomson's idea that the atomic electrons moved in circles around the atom's center. That meant that they revolved around the nucleus much as the constituents of the rings of Saturn revolve around the planet. But Saturnian atoms are not stable because, unlike the particles making up Saturn's rings, electrons repel one another. The slightest jarring would tear Rutherford's model atoms apart.

Moreover, the atoms of the lightest elements would lose energy very quickly by radiation. The worst case would be hydrogen, which on the nuclear model could have only one electron since the next heavier atom, helium, by definition had only two. Even a ring of two has some protection from radiation since each electron absorbs some of the energy radiated by the other. The single electron of the hydrogen atom would radiate without receiving any energy in return and spiral quickly into its nucleus. According to Rutherford's model, there should be no hydrogen in the universe. Explaining why hydrogen exists became the burning passion of a Danish postdoctoral student in Rutherford's laboratory named Niels Bohr.

The average difference of atomic weight between neighboring elements in the lower reaches of the periodic table of the elements is about two. Those who accepted Rutherford's rule $n = A/2$ might reasonably expect that the atoms of nearest neighbors there differed by a single electron. Working out this relation became the passion of a research student from Oxford named Henry Moseley. By placing the seat of radioactivity in the nucleus and that of ionization in the electronic rings, Rutherford distinguished pictorially between processes lumped together in Thomson's atom and opened the way to an understanding of the differences and similarities of the radioelements. This understanding was brought close by the work of a postdoctoral student from Hungary named Georg von Hevesy and clinched by Soddy, then a professor in Glasgow, in 1913. Bohr, Moseley, and Hevesy were all together in Rutherford's laboratory in 1912.

Niels Bohr had come to England in the hope of working with J. J. Thomson. "I considered first of all Cambridge as a center of physics," he later said of his decision to study there, "and Thomson as a most wonderful man, a genius, who showed the way for everybody." Bohr arrived in September 1911, just after finishing his doctoral thesis at the University of Copenhagen. He immediately wrote his fiancée. "I found myself rejoicing this morning, when I stood outside a shop and by chance happened to read the address 'Cambridge' over the door." Thomson received him kindly. "You should know what it was for me to talk to such a man," Bohr continued. "I think he thought there was something in what I said." The "something" contained some criticisms of Thomson's work. The collaboration Bohr had hoped for did not materialize. Thomson had no appetite for investigating his own errors and could not easily understand Bohr's soft-spoken and uncertain English. After two semesters at Cambridge, which he spent profitably, Bohr went to Rutherford at Manchester to learn something about the experimental side of radioactivity. He immediately became involved with the nuclear atom.

Bohr had an odd turn of mind, perhaps a consequence of the philosophy he imbibed at his parents' dinner table. (His father, a professor of physiology at the University of Copenhagen, belonged to a club of intellectuals that included the reigning philosopher in Denmark.) Bohr liked

Rutherford's model for just the reason that most physicists did not—for its radical instability. Since no physical principle fixed its diameter and its rings were altogether unstable, some additional assumption was necessary to determine its size, explain its endurance, and give the young physicist who contrived a successful assumption a chance for fame and fortune. By the summer of 1912 Bohr had a good idea that the assumption had something to do with Planck's radiation theory. He wrote his brother: "It could be that I have perhaps found out a little bit about the structure of atoms. . . . If I'm right, it would not be an indication of the nature of a possibility (like J. J. Thomson's theory) but perhaps a little piece of reality."

The little piece of reality was the postulate that the diameters of the rings of the nuclear atom were fixed by the size of the energy elements, or quanta, that Planck had introduced in 1900. Bohr decreed that the product of an electron's mass, velocity, and distance from the nucleus was to be exactly one quantum. On his own say-so, Bohr freed electrons that satisfied this condition from their ordinary need to radiate when they traveled in circles. On the same basis—his own say-so—he ordered that atomic electrons in orbits that obeyed his quantum condition not respond to forces that, on accepted physical theory, should have pulled light atoms apart. Theorists can do this sort of thing.

After returning to Denmark, Bohr discovered that his quantized version of Rutherford's model of the atom could predict the colors of the lines in the spectrum of hydrogen and singly ionized helium. He had only to allow additional protected orbits (or, as he called them, "stationary states") for electrons in atoms. These orbits satisfied the condition that the product of the electron's mass, velocity, and distance from the nucleus be equal to two, three, four, or more quanta. According to Bohr, an electron does not radiate in a stationary state. Spectral lines arise only during the transition of an

text continues on page 73

BOHR'S ATOMIC THEORY

ccording to one of several ways in which Planck's theory of radiation was understood around 1910, a quantized electron bound into an atom did not enjoy the freedom that a corpuscle had in Thomson's model. In the laissez-faire world of English physics, corpuscles obeyed the ordinary laws of physics but otherwise could circulate at whatever distance they pleased from the center of the atom. Bohr and others introduced the further constraint that each electron could not have more than one quantum of "action." Action is a definite physical quantity, the product of the momentum (the mass times the velocity of a particle) and the distance over which the momentum acts.

Planck had been led to assign a minimum value to this product, to which he gave the symbol h; if the circumference of the orbit $2\pi r$ is taken to be the relevant distance, the new rule amounted to $2\pi mvr = h$. Bohr eventually imposed just this rule on the electrons in his version of Rutherford's atom. Together with the ordinary laws of physics, which, with one exception, he also applied to the orbits, the new rule determined the dimensions of atoms from the basic constants e, m, and h. The exception to his application of the ordinary laws was to decree that electrons for which $2\pi mvr = h$ were so rigidly held, by a mechanism he could not specify, that they neither radiated energy nor deviated from their orbits.

text continued from page 71

electron from one stationary state to another, the so-called "quantum jump." The greater the jump, the bluer the line.

Bohr sent his paper to Rutherford to forward to an English journal. Rutherford's reply indicates the weakness of his strength.

> The mixture of Planck's ideas with the old mechanics makes it very difficult to form a physical idea [that is, picture] of the basis of it all. There appears to me one grave difficulty in your hypothesis, which I have no doubt you fully realize, namely, how does an electron decide what frequency it is going to vibrate at [that is, what color of light it will emit] when it passes from one stationary state to the other? It seems to me that you would have to assume that the electron knows beforehand when it is going to stop.

Moseley at his college laboratory in Oxford just before he went to work for Rutherford in 1910.

Under criticism like this, Bohr limited even further the authority of ordinary reasoning over the atom. The jumps of electrons had nothing to do with physical vibration; their activities during their leaps could not be described; in short, physicists' usual notions of space, time, and motion did not apply to most of the activities of electrons bound in atoms.

When Einstein first heard about Bohr's radical separation of the motions of electrons from the color of the light they emit, he declared himself persuaded. His informant, Hevesy, then traveling in Europe on vacation, later told Rutherford of Einstein's reaction: "'Should Bohr's theory be right, it is of the greatest importance.' When I told him about [experiments confirming Bohr's prediction about the lines of ionized helium] the big eyes of Einstein got bigger still and he told me, 'Then it is one of the greatest discoveries.'" In the form given it by Bohr, Rutherford's model became the vehicle for the further development of quantum theory as well as of atomic physics. The nuclear model, too, was one of the greatest discoveries. Among many other consequences, when quantized by Bohr it forced physicists to renounce the sort of intuitive pictures of the insides of atoms that guided the thinking of Thomson and Rutherford. One quality of a successful physical theory is that it points the way to its own replacement.

Like Bohr, Henry Moseley came from an academic family. Both his father and grandfather were fellows of the Royal Society and professors, the grandfather in London, the father at Oxford, where Harry (as his family and his few friends called him) grew up. In 1910, having been graduated without much distinction from Oxford, he went to Manchester as a demonstrator and started (as he put it in his kindly way) "teaching idiots elements." He felt himself not only above the students, but also at least the equal of Rutherford, whose tea-time conversation of slang, banter, and wisecracks he judged more suitable to a caricature of a colonial than to a professor of physics.

Moseley's arrogance did him and physics a good turn. Only people with great self-confidence, like Moseley and the gentle but stubborn Bohr, could go their own way in Rutherford's laboratory; most of the research students or assistants, like Marsden and Geiger, worked on problems in radioactivity assigned to them by the professor. Moseley began by doing what he was told. But after two years of this regime, when he had shown his ability and held the John Harling fellowship, he felt ready to stand up to Rutherford and to choose his own research projects. Although Rutherford at first opposed this independence, he came to regard Moseley as the best of his students—apart from Bohr.

Moseley chose to work on X rays, which, in 1912, had once again become a lively subject of research. That year Max von Laue and his associates in Munich showed that X rays passed through a crystal behave like light sent through a fine grating. Their experiment was followed up in England by William Lawrence Bragg, a research student in Cambridge, and his father, William Henry Bragg, a great friend of Rutherford's and professor of physics at the University of Leeds. The Braggs soon worked out a way to get the X-ray spectrum of atoms by reflection from a crystal surface. These discoveries provided the long-sought evidence that X rays are light of very high frequency (that is, of a "color" far beyond the ultraviolet). Moseley's interest soon turned from investigating the nature of the rays to extracting from their spectra clues to the constitution of atoms. He therefore returned in a roundabout way to a problem of central interest to Rutherford.

Results came thick and fast. Moseley compared the frequencies of the most penetrating X rays given out by 10 of the elements in the periodic table from calcium to zinc. These frequencies increased from one element to the next in an astonishingly simple way. They involved a whole number, now designated Z, that went up by one unit between nearest neighbors in the table of elements. Moseley interpreted Z as the element's place in the table starting with hydrogen at one, helium at two, and so on. Rutherford's model offered a simple representation of the physical meaning of Z: it is the charge on the nucleus.

By identifying an element by the value of Z indicated by its X-ray spectrum, Moseley could analyze in an instant samples of possible new elements that chemists had taken years to construct. One hopeful, Georges Urbain, a distinguished French chemist, came from Paris grasping a vial containing what he claimed to be a new element to which he had given the name "celtium." Moseley took its spectrum and declared, in what he called "dog French," that it was only a mixture of known elements. Urbain taught him something too, however. Moseley had been so fully imbued with the British system of modeling in physics and so little instructed in anything else that it had not occurred to him that the French might have their own way of doing things. He shared this revelation with Rutherford. "[Their] point of view is essentially different from the English. Where we try to find models or analogies, they are quite content with laws." Rutherford knew this fact very well. The English method had helped him to outrun the Curies and Becquerel.

Moseley's pass through the periodic table confirmed that the chemists had missed (but had left spaces for) four elements between aluminum ($Z = 13$) and gold ($Z = 79$). Two of them do not exist naturally; the other two duly came to light, one of them, hafnium, in Bohr's institute in Copenhagen in 1922, just in time for him to announce it in his Nobel prize lecture. Moseley's examination of the table also confirmed the chemists' wisdom in not following slavishly the principle of ordering the table by weight. At three places below gold—at potassium/argon, cobalt/nickel, and iodine/tellurium—they had had to place the heavier element first in order to get both to fall into the right chemical families. For many years chemists had hoped that more refined measurements would reveal errors in the accepted weights and restore the principle on which the periodic table was built.

The high frequency spectra followed atomic number *Z*, not atomic weight *A*. It appeared that the builders of the periodic table had been lucky: *A* is a good but not a perfect stand-in for *Z*. Moseley's demonstration of the precedence of *Z* over *A* was the climax of the inquiry into atomic structure begun by Thomson and advanced by Rutherford. Although the non-English-speaking world took little interest in the models on which they based their reasoning, all physicists and chemists soon accepted their simple and elegant result.

The fall of atomic weight as an indicator of chemical properties solved the serious problem of the overpopulation of radioelements. Chemists had worked hard to find chemical differences between products that seemed chemically similar but, according to the Rutherford-Soddy theory, had to have different atomic weights. Examples were thorium and radiothorium, known to differ by at least four mass units, and thorium and Boltwood's ionium, the parent of radium. When do you declare a difficulty an impossibility? The first chemists to surrender were Americans, who declared in 1907 that their failure to detach radiothorium from thorium indicated not their incompetence but the elements' inseparability. A Viennese chemist who had exhausted himself trying to split ionium from thorium thereupon declared them inseparable too, a conclusion favorably received by other chemists who had suffered similar frustrations. Soddy summarized the position in 1910: the inseparable pairs were "no mere chemical analogs [very similar in chemical properties] but chemical identities."

From this identity a horrible conclusion followed. Soddy again: "Chemical homogeneity is no longer a guarantee that any supposed element is not a mixture of several of different atomic weight, or that any atomic weight is not

text continues on page 79

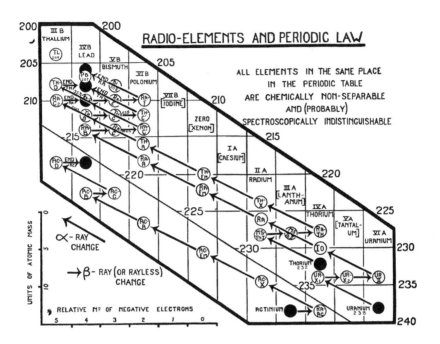

In this chart of isotopes and transformations dating from 1913, the decay from thorium begins at the black circle at A = 232. Emission of an alpha particle moves its chemistry two places to the left and its weight four units up; hence the diagonal arrow pointing to MsThI (mesothorium I). Two beta decays move the product chemically two places to the right, back to thorium, but four mass units lighter than it was at the start. Then come five successive alpha emissions resulting in a mass loss of twenty, followed by a beta emission to the end product, a lead isotope with A = 208. The series beginning with uranium and actinium have similar histories. All products in the same vertical columns are isotopes of the same element.

text continued from page 77

a mean number." Homogeneity, that is, perfect agreement in chemical properties, was consistent with disagreement in physical properties, notably weight and radioactivity. The mean weight of an element meant nothing. It was merely the average of the weights of chemically identical elements differing in other respects. Later Soddy invented the term "isotope" to indicate any of the several physically different elements occupying the same place in the periodic table.

It remained to relate the radioelements to their places. Soddy observed that the loss of an alpha particle appeared to move an element two places to the left in the periodic table. In 1913 he and three other chemists—Hevesy, a German (Kasimir Fajans), and a Scot (A. S. Russell), all of whom had spent time with Rutherford in Manchester— enunciated the corresponding rule for beta emission. An element losing a beta particle moves one place to the right. On this understanding, thorium emits an alpha particle to become mesothorium I (Hahn's discovery), an element two places to the left and therefore isotopic with radium; mesothorium I then goes one step to the right by a beta emission, producing another mesothorium (likewise a discovery of Hahn's), which takes another step to the right in producing an element isotopic with thorium. This element, radiothorium, gives off an alpha particle in becoming thorium X, which must therefore be isotopic with mesothorium I and radium. And so it goes with the uranium and actinium series as well. What could be clearer?

These displacement rules found an immediate and easy explanation on the basis of the nuclear model and the concept of atomic number. The loss of an alpha particle from the nucleus decreases Z by two; the loss of a beta particle augments Z by one; an alpha followed by two betas restores the original value of Z but not, of course, the original value of A. The radioelement produced in this manner has the same chemical properties as its ancestor three generations removed, but different physical properties.

Some of Rutherford's peers at the Solvay Congress held in Brussels in 1911 to discuss problems of radiation and the quantum. Rutherford is standing third from the right, two places to the right of Albert Einstein and behind Marie Curie.

In the dazzling years between the discovery of radioactive disintegration and the working out of the concepts of isotope and atomic number, Rutherford had made, or inspired others to make, a series of experimental and theoretical discoveries for which there are few parallels in the history of science. It was the work of young men. Rutherford himself had just turned 30 when he began collaborating with Soddy, then only 24. Geiger was but 25, Bohr, Hahn, and Hevesy 26, and Moseley 23 when they came under Rutherford's influence.

Rutherford's performance as discoverer and research director brought him all sorts of honors and, what is even harder to attain, the enduring friendship of his students and junior associates. In 1914 he was knighted. Hevesy telegraphed congratulations. Rutherford acknowledged that the honor was "very satisfactory" but also "a little embarrassing for a relatively youthful and impecunious Professor." Rutherford's little daughter Eileen, his only child, also doubted. "She is of the opinion that neither of her parents has the 'swank' and natural dignity for such decorations." In answer to Hahn's congratulations, Rutherford wrote of his pleasure at his former students' pleasure in "this recognition of my labour in the past" and of his amusement by the ceremony at Buckingham Palace, to which he had to wear a special uniform complete with sword. Quite a get-up for a man who, when a photographer came to take his picture in his laboratory at McGill, had had to borrow a pair of white cuffs from the better dressed Hahn.

Not yet 43, Rutherford had arrived at the height of his profession and had reproduced himself in the form of half a dozen talented research students. Soddy, Hahn, Bohr, and Hevesy all won Nobel prizes. Moseley would have won one also, doubtless before any of the others, had it not been for World War I.

This advertisement of 1914 was the best known and probably the most effective recruiting poster for the British army during World War I. Later the U.S. Army commissioned a similar poster, with Uncle Sam in the leading role.

War and the Promotion of Science

The laws of physics are supposed to be the same every-where. They are global, even universal. Physicists liked to believe that they shared in this quality, that minds fortified by the principles of their science could not be swayed by the jingoism that corrupted their fellow countrymen. This belief was put to the test in September 1914, when the German army, carrying out a long-matured plan, swept through Belgium and into France in a Blitzkrieg, or light-ning war, designed to conquer before the enemy could mobilize its defense. Stopped outside Paris by French and British forces, the Germans dug in, opposed by allied trenches that eventually stretched in an unbroken line from the English Channel to Switzerland. The Blitzkrieg became a Sitzkrieg, a siege war, a war of attrition. Troops on both sides who manned these trenches, and their comrades who fought in Italy, Austria-Hungary, Russia, and Turkey, spent most of their time in the mud exchanging artillery barrages. That was the good part. From time to time, when the generals could not restrain their frustration and stupidity, they ordered the men from the mud to attack the strongly entrenched positions of the enemy.

The gains from the barrages and the attacks usually did not exceed a few hundred yards. The cost per yard in men and materiel is as hard to imagine as the number of dollars in the national debt or the number of stars in the universe. On July 1, 1916, in the first of the battles of the Somme, which were to last into November, the British suffered the loss of over 60,000 men killed, maimed, or wounded. The firing of 1,500,000 artillery rounds had not softened the enemy's positions. When the insane enterprise of overrunning the German trenches was finally abandoned 20 weeks later, the British and the Germans had each suffered 420,000 casualties. The mess has never been cleaned up. To this day, the farmers of northern France continue to harvest fragments of bodies and bits of shell. They set aside intact explosives near back roads for pickup and demolition. Every day we hear milder echoes of the Great War on radio and television. At the war's end, Norwegian meteorologists introduced the concept of the weather front, an extended boundary across which hot and cold air contend for supremacy, in explicit analogy to the pointless stymied struggle on the battlefield.

The war killed, maimed, and destroyed much more efficiently than any previous conflict because it was the first fully to mobilize the inventions and productivity of modern technological societies. It was also the first war during which scientific research and industrial development produced new weapons that decisively affected the course of events. This war work came to occupy almost all physicists and chemists, and many scientists from other disciplines, on both sides of the barbed wire. During the first 16 months or so of the war, however, the generals—demonstrating their invincible stupidity—wasted their scientific manpower in the trenches. Several of Rutherford's students spent time at the front, and a few died there.

Professors too old for the front did not immediately engage in war work either. Instead they spent their time impotently hurling insults, proving that the vaunted internationalism of science did not extend to its senior practitioners. The first shot in this propaganda war was fired by 93 German intellectuals, including Max Planck and nine other past or future Nobel laureates. They repudiated the reports that their troops had committed atrocities during the Blitzkrieg in Belgium. More irritating to them even than the accusation of brutality ("war is war") was the slander, as they saw it, that their men, commanded by young officers they had educated, had willfully and unnecessarily destroyed treasures of art and science. A country that had given birth to a Beethoven and a Goethe, they said, knew how to respect the cultural heritage of Europe. The appeal

This rangefinder is typical of the equipment that Britain and France imported from Germany before the war. It was made by the German optical works of Zeiss, which also supplied microscopes to the world.

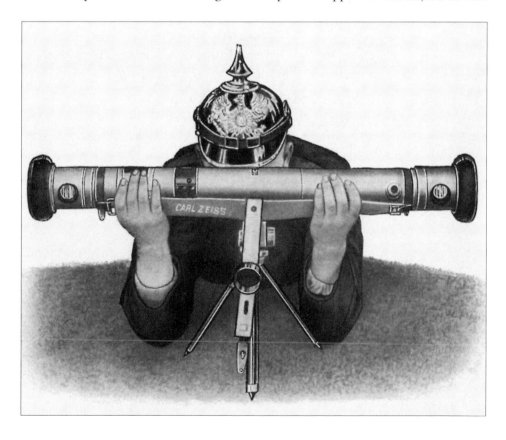

of the 93 was supported by a declaration by no fewer than 3,016 university-level lecturers.

These manifestos disgusted the Allies, who knew what had happened in Belgium. They accused the signers of taking on faith, on the assurance of their government, statements about which, as scientists, they should have withheld judgment. But it is easy to fall from high ground. In their turn, Belgian, British, French, and Italian scientists mocked German pretensions to culture and agreed to keep the Huns out of world science once the war was won.

When the Americans decided to join the Allied cause, they sold war bonds with the slogan, "a German B.A. = Bachelor of Atrocities." But if the Germans were uncivilized, how had they managed to dominate much of science before the war? Better organization was the answer given by the Allies. And—the argument continued—because Germans were good only at organization, they could not have led the intellectual advance of science. They lacked the effervescence of the Latin mind, and the playful boldness of the English. French physicists who developed this unpromising line of thought twisted the facts to conclude that the English mode of visualizing physical theories, which they had condemned as crude and babyish, agreed better with the clarity of their own thinking than the crude methods of the Germans, which they had praised before the war. William Ramsay, who had cheerfully pocketed the radium lent him by the Viennese seven years earlier, yelled among the loudest in the Allied war of words against Austro-German science.

There were voices of reason and acts of generosity amid the collapse of scientific internationalism. The grand old physicist Lorentz, who, as a citizen of the neutral Netherlands, could afford not to take sides, and who knew very well what had happened in neighboring Belgium, convinced Planck to withdraw his endorsement of the "Manifesto of the 93." Planck was the only signatory to do so during the war and he became the voice of moderation in the Berlin Academy of Sciences. Thomson, as president of the Royal Society, pursued a similar path, and squelched an absurd attempt to remove Rutherford's old patron Arthur Schuster from his position as the Society's secretary because of his German origin. Both Planck and Thomson also successfully opposed efforts to oust foreign members who were citizens of enemy powers from the Berlin Academy and the Royal Society.

Rutherford, who had good reason not to think England perfect in every respect, did not join in the patriotic excess. He knew that the war had not transmuted his old friends Hahn and Geiger into monsters. Geiger did his best to make life easier for British scientists detained in Germany at the outbreak of war or captured during the course of it. The instruments he supplied James Chadwick, one of Rutherford's most promising research students who had gone to study in Berlin in 1913, enabled Chadwick to do some respectable physics during his captivity and to prepare himself for a successful postwar stint at the Cavendish. For a time Rutherford kept up with the activities of his former students in Germany via letters forwarded from Copenhagen to Bohr, who spent 1915 and 1916 in Manchester.

Young men poured from the universities and engineering schools into the battlefield mud. A few examples will illustrate the unprecedented mobilization of the sons of Europe's cultured classes. The total enrollment of the German technical schools was 12,000 in the last prewar term and 2,000 six months later. The École normale supérieure, the largest nursery for young scientists in France, emptied; it became a hospital. The entering class of 1914, 80 strong, went to war immediately after matriculation: 20 were killed, 18 wounded. Some 160 of the older boys joined their juniors: half were killed, 64 wounded. Total enrollments in French universities fell by 75 percent during the first war years.

British universities pushed staff and students into battle by guaranteeing readmission after hostilities without loss of seniority or financial support. The pressure to enlist was hard to resist. The student body at Oxford fell from 3,000 to 300. About two-thirds of the students at Oxford and Cambridge went directly to the front, usually as junior officers; their average time of survival there was 30 days. Almost all the research staff of the Cavendish Laboratory had either left for the war by 1915 or were drilling daily in the Officers Training Corps. Rutherford's laboratory in Manchester suffered a similar evacuation.

After several months of Sitzkrieg, the young Allied scientists and engineers who had plunged into the trenches gradually withdrew behind the lines. Two main considerations forced their retreat: a vacuum in the stock of strategic, high-tech items previously imported entirely from Germany or Austria, and a yellow gas that rolled across the

Tethered balloons suspended men over the battlefield in baskets to observe enemy movements and spot aircraft and gun emplacements. They needed good binoculars of the kind previously imported from Germany.

battlefield at Ypres in April 1915. War planners awakened to the ability of chemists and physicists to invent substitutes for scarce items and to counter and worsen the effects of chemical warfare.

The strategic shortages were humiliating as well as menacing. Britain and France could not make optical glass for binoculars and periscopes, starters for automobile and aircraft engines, dyes for military uniforms, or apparatus for laboratory work. All these, and much more, they had imported from Germany before the war. The Germans, on their side, were cut off from rubber and other raw materials by the British blockade of continental ports. So important were binoculars to the allies that the British arranged with the Germans to exchange rubber for optical glass. The deal did not materialize, however, because the Allies taught themselves how to make the necessary glass, and many other things, before supplies ran out. The method was simplicity itself. Physicists and chemists reassigned to war work in industrial and university laboratories adapted and improved German patents and techniques. Brains, organization, and urgency worked wonders. By 1916 both the French and the British could make many things that they had previously ordered from Germany. They paraded their achievement in several exhibitions of technical materials and apparatus in London and Paris during the war.

The Sitzkrieg made the artillery, which was needed to soften the enemy's positions, deliver poison gas behind its lines, and knock out its guns, into the leading combat arm. Many technical resources were devoted to locating targets and improving the aim of the guns. Young Bragg and Ernest Marsden spent several years at the front directing the operation of devices built and perfected by physicists to pinpoint enemy artillery by recording and analyzing the sound made by shells passing overhead. Scientists launched balloons with recording devices to monitor the state of the wind at various heights over the battlefield. With the information supplied by Bragg's men and by battlefield meteorologists, British gunners could destroy enemy positions with an accuracy the Germans could not match. Other battlefield employment of scientists included laying out and maintaining electrical power supplies and telephone services. Moseley went into a telephone unit in the Royal Engineers. He was killed in battle in 1915 while telephoning from the front line for help.

Most of the foreign students who had worked in Rutherford's laboratory at McGill or Manchester were citizens of the Central Powers (as the Austro-German alliance was called). The main exception, Bohr, was officially neutral. The others engaged in hostilities against the Allies. Geiger served as an artillery officer, suffered wounds, and returned to the front. Hahn helped to develop, test, and use poison gas. Hevesy, caught by the war on a visit to Vienna, was inducted into the Austro-Hungarian army. To complete the roster of the younger Germans mentioned so far, Laue, whose work had inspired the Braggs', spent the war behind the front working on radio communications for the military.

The senior scientists who have appeared in our story played their parts behind the lines—except for Marie Curie, who organized a medical X ray service and for a time drove an ambulance around the front. Planck continued to try to restrain his rabid colleagues even after his elder son, a promising physicist, had been killed in battle. Becquerel and Pierre Curie had died before the war. Einstein, then occupying a prestigious professorship in Berlin, clung to pacifism. Soddy directed war work in his laboratory at the University of Aberdeen. Ramsay ranted and raved against the Huns, who had taught him chemistry, before he died a natural death in 1916. Rayleigh headed the British War Office's Committee on Explosives. C. T. R. Wilson devised ways to protect military balloons from atmospheric electricity. The elder Bragg and Rutherford led the attack of British physicists on scientific problems associated with the war and

themselves worked on the most pressing of them: the defeat of the submarine, the U-boat.

The Allied blockade had proved so successful that the Germans had to devise substitute raw materials and, where that was not possible, import the materials they needed by submarine. The effective blockade strengthened the hand of the German military, who called for all-out war, the use of poison gas, and the torpedoing of every vessel on the high seas. This last policy was very risky, as it threatened to bring the United States, which at first tried to practice neutrality, into the war. And so it did, but not before the German navy had taken a devastating toll on Allied shipping. Locating submerged submarines by the sounds they emitted became the highest priority for the Allies, including the United States. To orient their new partner, the French and British sent a delegation of their leading scientists to Washington in May 1917.

The leader of the British delegation was Rutherford. He passed through Paris on his way to the United States to coordinate the Allied mission and to see for himself what French physicists were doing. He met his old friend Paul Langevin,

A scientist at the Western front, Madame Curie sits in a car she outfitted with X-ray apparatus and drove around the battlefield during the war.

who was working on submarine detection; Marie Curie, "looking rather gray and worn and tired," still engaged in radiology; and the members of the French delegation. When they arrived in Washington, the joint mission did an extraordinary, perhaps an unprecedented, thing: they disclosed the state of Allied accomplishments and setbacks in the application of science to war in full detail. The Americans were surprised at the progress made and eager to put their technical and productive resources—far greater than the French and British possessed—behind further development.

The many meetings with scientists, ambassadors, and American officials tested the strength even of Rutherford. "We had breakfast in pyjamas on Sunday morning—grapefruit and tea—" he wrote, "and then discussed organization with Millikan and Co." In peacetime, Robert Millikan was a physicist whose re-measurement of the charge on the electron brought Thomson's method into agreement with Rutherford's, and, eventually, a Nobel prize for himself. During the war, Millikan was a senior member of the National Research Council, the central U.S. agency set up for drafting scientists into war work. "At 12 [Rutherford's account of his day continues] we called on the British ambassador . . . [then] to the Bureau of Standards. The weather is getting pretty warm [a typical understatement for "very hot"] but I sleep well in pyjamas without a sheet and generally my constitution stands well the strain of so many lunches and dinners."

Among the scientists with whom Rutherford spoke was his old friend Boltwood, who had been pro-German before the United States entered the war but now was working on the detection of submarines. This was Rutherford's special province, too. For two years or so he had been studying how sound moved through water in tanks he had had installed in the basement of his laboratory in Manchester. He approached the problem theoretically as well as experi-

text continues on page 94

Most of the methods investigated for detecting submarines during World War I used the human ear improved by devices ("hydrophones") for picking up sound at sea. Typically, a patrol boat carried or towed two phones symmetrically placed on either side of its keel. Air-filled tubes ran from the port phone to the left ear of the listener, and from the starboard phone to the right ear. To determine the direction from which an underwater sound came, the listener turned the phones until the noise levels in the two ears became equal. He then knew that the source of the noise lay on the perpendicular bisector of the line joining the phones. To attack the submarine, the patrol boat cruised in the direction determined by the listener. Since the sound would grow stronger as the boat approached its target, and then diminish if it overshot the mark, its crew would know when and where to drop its depth charges. Rutherford and his colleagues had many practical problems to overcome before this passive system could be made operational, in particular, designing phones and tubes able to amplify weak underwater sounds and finding a way to block out noises arising from the patrol boat's own machinery.

A British sailor listening to sounds from hydrophones towed by his ship. He directs changes of course so as to maximize the sound and equalize its intensity in his ears.

text continued from page 92

mentally, arming himself with the world's bible on acoustics, the voluminous treatise composed by Lord Rayleigh before he began to weigh the air. Rutherford recruited A. B. Wood, who had been a research student in Manchester at the same time as Bohr and Moseley, to test his ideas at a naval station in Scotland. The elder Bragg soon took charge of the scientific side of the work there. The outcome was the equipping of British submarines with hydrophones (metal plates connected up to act like telephones) able to detect the presence and determine the direction of U-boats. Unfortunately the listening submarine had to stop to hear, since the noise of its own engines confused its hydrophones. The problem of self-noise and sea noise afflicted hydrophones carried by surface vessels even more strongly.

The hydrophone method had the additional disadvantage of being passive. It depended on noises emitted by the enemy. An active approach—sending out sound waves and monitoring their reflection from the object of search—had much to recommend it. It could work even when the enemy made no noise and could operate at a special frequency that distinguished it from the search ship's sounds. But it also required considerable energy, since the target would reflect back only a very small fraction of the sound emitted by the searcher. Rutherford and Langevin recognized that only sound of very high frequencies, far above the audible range, could travel in water without unacceptable loss of energy. To generate this "ultra sound," both Rutherford and Langevin used a device based on an effect discovered by Pierre Curie and his brother Paul.

The Curie brothers had found that certain crystals, quartz, for example, change shape when electrified; under a rapidly changing electrical force, the crystal vibrates with equal rapidity. (This is the principle of modern quartz timepieces.) R. W. Boyle, yet another of Rutherford's old students from his McGill days, was put to work developing Rutherford's ideas for active detection of submarines. The

technique, which became practicable only at the war's end, is the basis of sonar, an instrument useful in peacetime to locate icebergs and oil deposits.

Rutherford's war work not only resulted in useful bits of hardware but also helped to demonstrate the navy's need for continuing scientific advice during peacetime. And not only the navy. The accomplishments of science during the war convinced the entire military, and much of industry, that science was essential to their mission. As the leading spirit of the National Research Council, the astronomer George Ellery Hale, put it, "the war had forced science to the front." World War I was a watershed in the relations between science, technology, government, and industry. In 1914, military establishments and industry had few research laboratories anywhere, and in England government contributed very little to the educational expenses of young scientists. After the war, today's pattern of support of study and research in science and engineering began to take

The officers and civilian scientists who served on the Admiralty Physics board in 1921. Rutherford is seated third from the left in the center row and J. J. Thomson sits to his left.

shape. Rutherford was both a promoter and a beneficiary of this new system of support. The wartime agencies established to mobilize scientific manpower survived hostilities as the Department of Scientific and Industrial Research. Rutherford served as an advisor to it and received financial support for his laboratory and students from it.

The propaganda war between scientists in the belligerent countries could not be silenced as easily as the artillery. Hale worked to set up the International Research Council, whose main purpose was to shut out members of the former Central Powers from participation in international scientific meetings and collaborations. It held its inaugural convention in 1918. At the insistence of the French and Belgians, the exclusion of Germany and Austria was affirmed. Rutherford and Lorentz tried to remove these exclusions; they succeeded in 1926, with a proposal made by Rutherford just after his election to the presidency of the Royal Society. He and most other Allied scientists already had resumed contact with their German and Austrian collaborators on an informal basis.

To Geiger, who wrote on May 18, 1918, to say that he had survived four years at the front, Rutherford replied that "I retain my old friendly feeling for my old researchers and hope that we may meet again when things have settled down to a more normal footing." Rutherford did more than make friendly noises. He initiated contact with Stefan Meyer, the head of the Viennese Institute that had lent him radium before the war. Meyer replied that he and his colleagues faced crippling financial circumstances—they could scarcely afford food let alone scientific books or apparatus. Rutherford responded by raising money from the Royal Society to buy the radium the Institute had lent him. The sum kept the Radium Institute going until Austria could again afford to maintain it.

During short breaks in his war work, Rutherford had managed to do a little research with his stock of Viennese radium and its decay products. One experiment, done during the last year of the war, was a master stroke. Before the war Marsden had noticed that when alpha particles passed through hydrogen, they knocked on other particles that traveled further in the gas than they did. These penetrating particles were evidently hydrogen nuclei, soon to be called "protons." When Rutherford tried the same experiment with nitrogen, he found the same fast particles that Marsden had detected in hydrogen. Where did the protons found in pure nitrogen come from? Rutherford proposed the bold explanation that they came from nitrogen nuclei.

As the great guns fell silent on the battlefield, nuclear projectiles were scoring their first big hits. Unlike the Geiger-Marsden experiments, in which the alpha particle is turned around by its encounter with a nucleus of gold or platinum, the bombarding alphas in Rutherford's new trials entered nitrogen nuclei, which thereupon emitted hydrogen. If the alpha stayed swallowed, then, according to the doctrine of atomic number, the lucky nitrogen nucleus would become one of oxygen.

At the war's end Rutherford had become the dominant force in British physics and a leading spokesman for British scientists. He had a civil title (Sir Ernest) and every sort of scientific honor. He had just provoked the transformation of matter. When, in 1919, J. J. Thomson announced that he would retire from the Cavendish professorship, there could be no doubt who should succeed him.

The Center of Physics

In 1919 Rutherford became the fourth Cavendish Professor of Experimental Physics at the University of Cambridge. Not quite 50 years had passed since the inauguration of the Cavendish laboratory under its first professor, James Clerk Maxwell. The half-century had transformed physics from a small specialty with insecure standing in universities and almost no ties to government or industry to a large enterprise with well-equipped institutes and departments in all the major universities and higher engineering schools, and an established place in industrial and government laboratories.

By 1914 the Cavendish's staff and research students numbered around 40. Hundreds of undergraduates studied there, training for careers in medicine, engineering, and teaching. (In Maxwell's time there had been only a handful of senior men at the laboratory and virtually no undergraduates.) Teaching and research ceased during the war. Rutherford's first business on taking over from Thomson was to oversee an orderly revitalization of the Cavendish. He soon brought it up to a new level of activity and achievement.

Rutherford drew on two sources, besides his own reputation and research projects, that his predecessor lacked.

Bohr and Rutherford relaxing during the 1920s.

One was a group of mature veterans eager to commence or continue careers in physics under a professor who seemed to be in direct contact with the creator of the universe. The other new source was financial. Industry and government (especially the recently formed Department of Scientific and Industrial Research, or DSIR) sponsored research students and gave money for scientific instruments much more readily after the war than before it. With good people and the money to support them, you did not need to be a Rutherford to succeed.

In one respect, however, Rutherford lacked something useful that Thomson possessed in an eminent degree. Although he had a sufficient grasp of mathematics to solve problems presented in his experiments on radioactivity and sound, he was no mathematician. Consequently he could not work out for himself the applications of the quantum theory of the atom, which, with the invention of quantum mechanics in 1925–26, became the domain of theorists well trained in mathematics. His resolution of the difficulty was to provide himself with a theorist. He tried to recruit Bohr, but Bohr preferred to remain in Copenhagen, where the government and leading foundations were building him an institute. Rutherford made do with Ralph Howard Fowler, who literally became a member of the family.

Fowler's early career encapsulated the experience of Cambridge men who graduated during the decade or so before the war. He obtained his B.A. in mathematics in 1911 and an appointment as a fellow of Trinity College, Cambridge, in October 1914 on the strength of the mathematical work he had done in the interim. Trinity was the college of the great mathematicians of the university, as well as of the Cavendish professors. But by October 1914 England had been at war for two months and Fowler had already joined in, as an artillery officer. Like Moseley, he was sent to Turkey; though wounded, he survived. After convalescence, he worked on ballistics and other mathematical-military problems, and in 1919 he returned to Cambridge to take up his fellowship. He was bound into an orbit around the Cavendish by Rutherford's daughter Eileen, whom he married in 1921. Fowler helped research students with problems in quantum physics and acted as a transmitter of developments at Bohr's institute in Copenhagen. In 1932 Fowler became professor of theoretical physics at Cambridge.

There were several other returning veterans who had long careers at the laboratory. Chadwick, returned from internment in Germany to a fellowship in Cambridge, became the Cavendish's Assistant Director for Research—a new post established with funds from the DSIR to relieve Rutherford of administrative burdens. Chadwick retained this demanding position until 1935, when he left for a professorship at the University of Liverpool. His administrative obligations did not keep him from research that brought him a Nobel prize.

John Cockcroft had been drawn to the study of physics by popular accounts of the discoveries of Thomson and Rutherford that he read as a boy; and he had the satisfaction of hearing introductory lectures from Rutherford at Manchester before he volunteered for the army. He became a signal officer in the Royal Artillery and participated in several major battles. He took a roundabout way back to Rutherford. After demobilization he returned to Manchester to study electrical engineering rather than physics, probably pursuing interests developed during his work as a signal officer. After obtaining his degree and doing a short stint at an industrial research laboratory (Metropolitan-Vickers), he went to Cambridge to study mathematics. In 1924 he started at the Cavendish. There he combined his miscellaneous training into a harmonious and productive whole. He developed an electrical machine for splitting atoms. It brought him a Nobel prize. He remained at Cambridge until World War II.

Patrick Maynard Stuart Blackett, eventually Baron Blackett, was the same age as Cockcroft. A naval cadet in 1914, he was assigned, though only 17, to duty on a cruiser as soon as war broke out. He served most of the war as a gunnery officer on antisubmarine vessels. He got to the Cavendish owing to a navy program to put a coat of culture on junior officers who had been rushed prematurely to active duty. This veneering consisted of a term in a Cambridge college. Blackett found it to his taste, resigned from the navy, won a college fellowship, and joined Rutherford's laboratory. His work, inspired by the progress C. T. R. Wilson had made in improving the cloud chamber (a device for making visible the paths of charged particles like alpha and beta rays), resulted in instruments to track cosmic rays. The subject was different from Chadwick's and Cockcroft's, but the outcome the same: a Nobel prize. To round out the litany, Wilson, who made his entire career at Cambridge, including the years 1925 to 1934 as a professor, received the Nobel prize in physics in 1927 for his invention of the cloud chamber.

Chadwick, Cockcroft, and Blackett were not only talented physicists but also strong administrators, good collaborators, and energetic organizers. All three built up important laboratories after leaving the Cavendish and led English physicists during World War II. They then became government advisors and spokesmen on all matters concerning science, government, and society. But strong as these men were, none of them could equal the powerhouse who enrolled in Cambridge for work toward a doctoral degree at the Cavendish in 1921. He was Peter Kapitsa, graduate of a Russian engineering school and already an expert on magnets. Brilliant, bold, and fearless, Kapitsa won Rutherford's respect and affection and, what few could believe, his support in raising research funds in excess of the total for all the other work done in the laboratory. The goal was to build a magnet much stronger than any previously built. It would be able to bend the paths of very energetic charged particles. The money, for staff as well as equipment, came mainly from the DSIR and the Royal Society.

In 1933 Kapitsa finished his laboratory, a freestanding building within the grounds of the Cavendish. He embellished its facade with the sculpture of a crocodile. "Crocodile" was Kapitsa's name for Rutherford from the first days of their acquaintance. "Crocodile often comes to see what I am doing," Kapitsa reported to his mother in December 1926.

> You are asking me to send Crocodile's photo to you. . . . Crocodile is a dangerous animal, and it is not so easy to photograph him. . . . Taking such liberties [joking] with Crocodile is generally very risky . . . and it seems I alone of the entire laboratory take a chance with such stunts. . . . Some six times in the past . . . I have heard such compliments from him as 'you fool,' 'jackass,' and the like. . . . I feel I am a member of a collective headed by Crocodile. I feel I am indeed turning one of the little wheels of European science.

Peter Kapitsa stands in front of the alternator he used to create huge magnetic fields at the Cavendish.

The reason for the nickname, which Kapitsa did not use to his boss's face, is that Russians regarded the crocodile with a mixture of awe and admiration. Kapitsa left the Cavendish in 1934 for a visit to the Soviet Union, which refused to allow him to return to England. He, too, won a Nobel prize.

Types such as by Kapitsa, Chadwick, Cockcroft, and Blackett did best with the blunt crocodile. Weaker or less convivial men had their troubles. Two of these, Wilson and Francis Aston, both holdovers from Thomson's era, kept themselves apart. Both liked to tinker with their apparatus without being bothered by collaborators. Aston's prestige would have given him a leading position in the laboratory if he had possessed the personality to claim it. He had spent the war working to improve military aircraft and returned to Cambridge as soon as he could, to a fellowship at Trinity. There he remained for the rest of his life. He quickly conquered the field he had opened with Thomson—the separa-

The Mond Laboratory in Cambridge bears a metal crocodile near its entrance to commemorate Kapitsa's nickname for Rutherford.

tion of isotopes by electric and magnetic forces. He thus confirmed the rule that the atomic weight of an element represents the average of the weights of its isotopes. In 1922 he and Soddy shared the Nobel prize in chemistry.

The weak without a prize could be miserable. Edmund Stoner suffered from self-doubt and diabetes. Nevertheless, he did well enough as an undergraduate at Cambridge, which he entered in 1918, for Rutherford to get him a DSIR grant to continue as a research student. He had trouble making his apparatus behave and his poor health limited his time in the laboratory. Stoner complained in his diary in March 1923 that Rutherford had became impatient, "apoplectic and annoying," over the lack of progress. "A blustering whirlwind, and unsympathetic, with a glaze of geniality. No doubt alright to really vigorous people, but good heavens! Undoubtedly one of the greatest experimental physicists, and with wonderful insight, but a man one can hardly respect, and certainly cannot love."

One of Stoner's troubles was that he was a closet theorist and not a gifted experimenter. Lectures given by Bohr in Cambridge in 1922 and papers from Bohr's institute gradually gave Stoner a focus. In 1924 he had an idea: "Had no sleep until 6 A.M.!! Wild thoughts on electronic structure, quantum numbers, intensities of [spectral] lines. . . . Very excited. . . . A day of grand theoretical excitement. . . . I may do something yet." He wrote an important paper. Chadwick and Kapitsa took note; they asked him to join the clubs they ran for the discussion of recent research. Stoner did not get a Nobel prize, but did secure, with Rutherford's help, a professorship at the University of Leeds. To make Rutherford shine upon you, you had only to do more work better than anyone else.

Although Rutherford's laboratory was a masculine, and sometimes a macho, place (he referred to his task as professor as "driv[ing] the boys along"), he had no objection to women research students. He had admired Harriet Brooks as "a woman of great charm and ability . . . [and] a welcome addition to any research laboratory." At Cambridge he supported the cause of women at the university. The group photographs of the Cavendish researchers show one woman each in 1921 and 1923 (out of 29 and 25 people, including Rutherford and Thomson) and two in 1932 (out of 39).

Just after Rutherford took up his professorship, the situation of women at Cambridge was very much improved by making them almost full members of the university. (Rutherford favored full equality with men; Thomson, who had spent his life in Cambridge, favored maintaining a few restrictions.) Although women had been allowed to study in the university and take examinations, they had not been able to receive degrees. To heighten the anomaly, those who took the final examinations in mathematics, the most prestigious in the university, were listed in order of merit, as were the men; but since the women could not earn degrees, their names appeared separately, with indications where they would have been placed had they been men. In 1890, the daughter of a philosopher and a suffragette placed above the best of the men; but this demonstration, which shocked the university, did not cause it to change its policy. It took the world war, in which women showed that they could do many jobs previously reserved for men, to force Cambridge to regularize the status of women.

As soon as his new administrative duties allowed, Rutherford returned to the line of research he had started in his last year at Manchester: the disintegration of light nuclei by irradiating them with alpha particles derived from the radium he had received from Vienna. (Rutherford favored RaC, a bismuth isotope, which emits especially fast alphas.) As usual, he made simple, even crude pictures of the collision that ejected protons from nuclei. He supposed that protons were nuclear constituents and that the bombarding alpha particles knocked them loose. Of what else might the nucleus be made? Rutherford thought that he knew part of

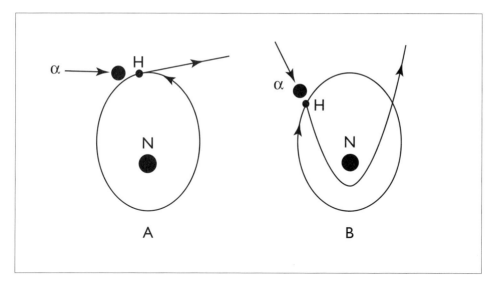

the answer, at least for the heavy, naturally radioactive elements. Assuming again that the particles ejected by a nucleus pre-existed in it, he placed alpha particles and electrons (to account for beta rays) in radioactive nuclei. To check on the constituents of light, stable nuclei, Rutherford asked Chadwick to join him in a search for other pieces knocked out of them by bombardment with alpha particles.

The first experiments turned up slow-moving fragments that appeared to have a positive charge of two units and a mass of three. Rutherford easily accommodated these X^{++} fragments in his developing notion of nuclear structure. He pictured the stable isotope of nitrogen (N), with atomic weight of 14 and nuclear charge of 7 ($^{14}N_7$), as four $^3X_2$ particles and two protons ($^1H_1$) somehow held together by three "deformed" electrons (represented by the minus signs in the following figure): the structure therefore had the required weight of $4 \cdot 3 + 2 = 14$ and the required charge of $4 \cdot 2 + 2 - 3 = 7$.

Rutherford and Chadwick postponed investigation of the X^{++} particles until they had examined the capacity of the alpha particles to eject protons from nuclei other than nitrogen. They succeeded with several elements of odd atomic

Rutherford's picture of nuclear collisions, drawn in 1920, shows the ways an alpha particle can knock a proton out of a nitrogen nucleus. Neither the proton nor its outlying orbit in fact exists.

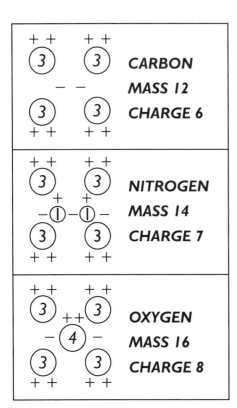

++   ++
(3)   (3)   **CARBON**
--   **MASS 12**
(3)   (3)   **CHARGE 6**
++   ++

++   ++
(3)   (3)   **NITROGEN**
+   +
-(1)-(1)-   **MASS 14**
(3)   (3)   **CHARGE 7**
++   ++

++   ++
(3) ++(3)   **OXYGEN**
-(4)-   **MASS 16**
(3)   (3)   **CHARGE 8**
++   ++

In this rough and wrong diagram dating from 1920, Rutherford composed nuclei of alpha particles, mass-three particles (X_3^{++}), and electrons so as to make up the observed values of A and Z. Thus oxygen contains one alpha particle, four X_3^{++}, and two electrons: $A = 4 \cdot 3 + 4 = 16$, $Z = 5 \cdot 2 - 2 = 8$.

weight from boron ($^{11}B_5$) to phosphorus ($^{31}P_{15}$). Rutherford emphasized that all the susceptible nuclei except nitrogen had atomic weights that could be expressed as 3 plus some multiple of four. That lent itself to picture making. Each susceptible nucleus should consist of three protons, a few electrons, and a number of alpha particles. Assuming that the three protons were relatively loosely held as "satellites" to the nuclear alpha particles, Rutherford imagined a productive (α, p) collision—an alpha (α) particle ejecting a proton (p)—as a sort of billiard game.

The X^{++} particles turned out to be a mistake. With Chadwick's help, Rutherford determined that they came not from the bombarded nucleus, but from the source. RaC gives off not only the alpha particles that Rutherford knew when he began to use it in his artillery, but also some faster ones that he had misidentified as pieces of nitrogen nuclei. The episode is worth recalling not to expose the errors of a great man but to illustrate that premature model making can indeed have the drawbacks deplored by the Curies. Rutherford's model of nitrogen was nonsense. The notion of alpha-proton (α, p) processes as billiard shots quickly went the way of the X^{++} particle. Somewhat later, the nuclear electron, whose existence seemed guaranteed by beta decay, also disappeared, and with it the reasonable assumption that the particles emitted in nuclear disintegration were present in the nucleus before the disintegration.

These last surprises came from following up another idea about nuclear structure that Rutherford had proposed in 1920. The close association of the electrons and protons located between the X^{++} and α particles in Rutherford's model of the nitrogen nucleus suggested a more intimate union, a particle with a mass of one and no charge. Such a particle, as Rutherford said, would be able to penetrate long distances through matter because, having no charge, it would not be caught up in the electrical forces from electrons and nuclei. It might well be able to penetrate even the heaviest nuclei, whose very high electric charge, some six times that of the weightiest element that Rutherford had disintegrated by the (α, p) process, would repel even the swiftest alpha particles. He made a few experiments to observe this neutral particle, but failed to find it. He had looked in the wrong place.

In 1930 two physicists in Berlin managed to excite a penetrating radiation by shining alpha particles on beryllium ($^9Be_4$), which Rutherford had not been able to disintegrate via (α, p). They used polonium as a source and supposed that the penetrating radiation was an energetic gamma ray (nuclear X ray). Irène Curie, working in her mother's laboratory in Paris, concurred; and, commanding the largest quantity of polonium in the world, soon created "beryllium rays" in abundance. In collaboration with her husband, Frédéric Joliot, she found that this radiation gave rise to fast protons when it fell on wax. They calculated that to produce this effect gamma rays would have to have an energy far in excess of that carried by the alpha particles that had stimulated their production.

In February 1932, a month after receiving news of this last experiment, Chadwick announced that Rutherford's neutral particle had been found, but not recognized, in Berlin and Paris. All energy relations fell into place if the beryllium radiation was not a gamma ray but a stream of particles with a weight near that of the proton. A colleague of Chadwick's at the Cavendish scavenged polonium from old tubes containing radium emanation that had been used in hospitals, and made a source almost as strong as the Parisian one. Chadwick then gave abundant evidence to show that the bombardment of beryllium gave rise to an (α, n) reaction, where n designates the neutron, one of the primary constituents of the atomic nucleus. The fast-moving neutrons knocked protons out of wax in a straightforward collision (not a nuclear reaction) with its hydrogen atoms. Since in an (α, n) reaction the target nucleus receives two additional charges, it moves two places to the right in the periodic table (thus beryllium to carbon), whereas (α, p), which brings a net change of one, moves it only one place (thus nitrogen to oxygen, phosphorus to sulfur).

After Curie and Joliot had recovered from their shock at missing so grand a detection as the neutron, they found something at least as good: a neutron *and* a positive electron from aluminum bombarded by alpha particles. (The positive electron, in the discovery of which Cambridge had a hand, came to light in 1932.) No one believed them and, indeed, they were not quite right. During experiments designed to answer their critics, they discovered that the neutron and the positive electron or positron (e^+) did not come out together. First the alpha particle worked an (α, n) reaction on the aluminum, changing it thereby to a radioactive isotope of phosphorus $^{30}P_{15}$, which quickly disintegrated by producing a positron to become a stable isotope of silicon. They thus made the very fine discovery that stable elements can be made radioactive. They brought one of their new radioactive creations to old Mme Curie, then dying of leukemia probably caused by her career with radioactivity. Joliot described the scene: "I can still see her taking [it] between her fingers, burnt and scarred by radium. . . . This was without doubt the last great moment of satisfaction in her life."

Another result of the discovery of artificial radioactivity is that isotopes can decay by the emission of positive as well as negative electrons. This last observation helped to kill Rutherford's idea of the pre-existence of alpha and beta rays in the nuclei that produced them. Theorists worked out that negative and positive beta radiation originated in the transformation in the nucleus of a neutron into a proton, or a proton into a neutron, respectively.

Rutherford had guessed correctly that neutrons would be prolific in provoking nuclear reactions. The leaders in this field were a group in Rome under Enrico Fermi, who used small-scale methods similar to the Joliot-Curies', and one under Ernest Lawrence at the University of California at Berkeley, who used a big new machine, the cyclotron. Various processes—(n,α), (n,p), $(n,2n)$—worked on elements throughout the periodic table. A large new research specialty arose, nuclear chemistry, which produced dozens of artificially active isotopes, some of which had value in the diagnosis and treatment of disease. The bombardment eventually reached the heaviest known element, uranium. At the end of 1938, just in time for exploitation in World War II, Hahn realized that, in contrast to all other nuclear reactions then known, uranium made artificially radioactive by swallowing neutrons did not necessarily end in a place close to itself in the periodic table. Sometimes a uranium nucleus that captured a neutron became so unstable that it split, or fissioned, into almost equal halves. Soon physicists realized that in fissioning a uranium nucleus also emits neutrons, making possible a chain reaction and an atomic bomb.

The beryllium radiation shone upon its investigators. Chadwick won the Nobel prize in physics for the neutron in 1935; Curie and Joliot, the chemistry prize for artificial radioactivity the same year, 1935; Fermi, the physics prize for neutron activation in 1938; Lawrence, the same for the cyclotron in 1939; and Hahn, the chemistry prize for fission in 1945.

In November 1927, in the anniversary address with which he began his second year as president of the Royal Society, Rutherford expressed a wish for a supply of "atoms and electrons which have an individual energy far tran-

text continues on page 113

The absorption of a neutron by an atom can have several consequences. One is the provocation of beta decay, as in the reactions investigated by Joliot and Curie in Paris; another is the ejection of a proton or an alpha particle, as studied notably by Fermi and his colleagues in Rome. All these processes shift the participating nucleus one or two places in the periodic table. A more dramatic disintegration also is possible: a nucleus can fission, that is, split into two almost equal parts, as a consequence of capturing a neutron. Uranium illustrates the range of possibilities. Natural uranium consists mainly of an isotope of weight 238 that decays spontaneously by alpha emission. But a nucleus of $^{238}U_{92}$ can also absorb a neutron via the Joliot-Curie reaction (n, e$^-$); the product evidently has the weight 239 and atomic number 93. It does not occur naturally and does not live very long when made: it decays spontaneously via beta emission to $^{239}Pu_{94}$, "plutonium-239," a long-lived isotope that made history in the bomb that destroyed Nagasaki. Both plutonium and its predecessor neptunium, first made at the Berkeley cyclotron, were named by their discoverers after the planets that follow Uranus in the solar system.

Natural uranium has another important isotope with weight 235. Like U-238, it decays slowly and naturally (it is the patriarch of the actinium family) and also can capture a neutron. When it does so, however, it explodes into fragments with atomic numbers in the middle reaches of the table of the elements. The explosion produces free neutrons as well, which might be swallowed by other U-235 nuclei, provoking more fissions; or they might fall into U-238 nuclei and stay there, causing the transformations that produce plutonium. Since more than 99 percent of natural uranium is U-238, neutrons produced by fission of U-235 have very little chance of causing further fissions before disappearing into U-238 nuclei or leaving the uranium sample entirely. If, however, enough pure U-235 can be assembled, a so-called critical mass, a chain reaction ensues that blows the mass to smithereens.

text continued from page 111

scending that of the alpha and beta-particles from radioactive bodies. I am hopeful that I may yet [he was 56] have my wish fulfilled, but it is obvious that many difficulties will have to be surmounted before this can be realized." Even as he spoke to the Royal Society, the men who were to supply what he wanted had come together at the Cavendish. They were John Cockcroft; an engineer on leave from Metropolitan-Vickers, T. E. Allibone; and an Irish research student on an 1851 Exhibition (the same scholarship Rutherford had had 30 years earlier), Ernest Walton.

The reason for seeking a man-made supply of fast particles for nuclear research was that natural sources provided too few. Since the nucleus occupies only a very small portion of its atom, the chance of hitting it with another nucleus—an alpha particle or a proton—is also very small. Rutherford estimated that only one or two alphas in a million caused a nuclear transformation in his experiments with nitrogen. If all the alphas from an entire gram of radium were absorbed in the nitrogen, they would produce less than a millionth of a cubic centimeter of hydrogen in a year. That was too little to allow easy study of collisions and rarer sorts of transformations. The need was not easy to satisfy. The bombarding particles had to be energetic as well as numerous. The energy required to provoke a nuclear reaction is about the same as the energy carried by the rays from naturally radioactive substances; a machine to shoot, say, an alpha particle into a nucleus had to be able to throw it with as much force as the nucleus could bring to bear to eject it. This energy was reckoned at 500,000 electron volts (eV).

The energy required to crack a nucleus thus appeared to be more than 50,000 times the energy needed to excite atomic electrons to emit light. No apparatus then existed for generating such a voltage or for holding it for any length of time. Therefore, several physicists, including Thomson, had toyed with the idea of acceleration in stages rather than in one large step, accumulating the energy on the particles rather than on the apparatus. The Cavendish physicists did not succeed in producing a stepwise accelerator. Instead, they were driven back to their original design by a head-on, though friendly, collision with a Russian emigré theorist, one of the great characters of modern physics, George Gamow.

Unable to gain permission to leave the Soviet Union in the mid-1920s, Gamow had rowed across the Black Sea to Turkey. From there he made his way to Bohr's institute in Copenhagen. He worked out a remarkable consequence of the then-new quantum mechanics: A particle can penetrate (or escape from) a nucleus with less energy than ordinary physics demanded. This so-called "tunnel effect," if it applied to a pool table, would have the astonishing and unpleasant consequence that occasionally balls would pass right through the cushions without breaking or tearing them in any way. Cockcroft recognized that if Gamow were right, Rutherford would have his wish.

Only 300,000 volts would be required to accelerate protons fast enough to have a good chance of penetrating boron nuclei. Rutherford, always skeptical about elaborate theories, allowed himself to be convinced. With the help of Allibone and others at Metro-Vick, Cockcroft and Walton filled a room at the Cavendish with the apparatus of electrical engineering, a scale-up of perhaps 100 in cost and size from the table-top instruments with which Rutherford had made his fundamental discoveries. It took more than three years after Gamow's intervention to perfect the equipment to generate and maintain 300,000 volts, to produce from hydrogen gas enough ions (that is, protons) for continuous acceleration, and to develop procedures for observing whatever might happen if the protons succeeded in cracking a nucleus.

By February 1932 Cockcroft and Walton had managed to push protons to 710,000 electron volts (710 keV). They announced that they would try for 800 keV. Rutherford grew impatient. He ordered them to stop fiddling and to look for

evidence of disintegration. But what evidence? Rutherford guessed that if Cockcroft and Walton hit a lithium nucleus with a proton they would make alpha particles. The lithium nucleus has a charge of three and its main isotope a weight of seven. Rutherford had in mind a reaction in which a fleeting combination of a lithium atom and a proton (with a total Z of 4 and A of 8) splits into two alpha particles (each with a Z of 2 and an A of 4). Cockcroft and Walton looked where they were directed. They saw the telltale flashes of alpha particles on the fluorescent screen they used as a detector. Rutherford came to look and confirmed that the flashes indicated alphas. "I should know an alpha-particle when I see one," he said later, "for I was in at the birth of the alpha-particle and have been observing them ever since."

The demonstration that man-made instruments could split an atomic nucleus made headlines all over the world.

text continues on page 118

The first Cockcroft-Walton machine, built in 1932, accelerated protons. The particles enter at the top of the pipe within the transparent cylinder in the right center of the photograph. The particles are then accelerated by the high potential generated by the stacks of condensers, which store electrical charge, and rectifiers, which change alternating into direct current, that fill the other cylinders. They strike their target within the curtained observation booth.

The problems of creating and maintaining high potentials for accelerating charged particles can be eliminated (and new ones introduced!) by accumulating energy on the particles rather than on the apparatus. One possibility is to accelerate particles in steps as schematized here: a stream of protons entering the apparatus at the left is drawn to the cathode K and thence accelerated by an electrical force between K and the negatively charged metal drift tube 1. ("Drift" signifies that, because there is no electric field within the tube, the protons sail through it with the velocity with which they entered.) On emerging from tube 1, they will be drawn back unless the negative charge on it has become positive. Suppose that a way can be found to change the polarity. Then the particles will accelerate toward tube 2, supposed negative; when they emerge from tube 2, its polarity must have changed for the acceleration to continue toward tube 3. The lengths of the drift tubes must be adjusted so that the time of transit through them is the same so that a radio oscillator can be used to regulate the fast-changing electrical force. The oscillator, with its connections to the tubes, is shown beneath the linac. The energy gained by the protons in passing through the apparatus is proportional to the number of drift tubes.

The linear accelerator is hard to realize in practice because it requires a long vacuum (the protons must not hit gas molecules) and finicky adjustment of the oscillating electric force; it first became practicable after World War II. A bent version of it, however, proved immediately successful. Protons enter this apparatus,

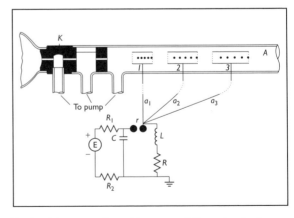

The Swedish engineer Gustav Ising proposed this version of a linac (linear accelerator) in 1933.

nicknamed a cyclotron, at its center. At that instant, they are accelerated across the gap between the shallow, hollow, semicircular cans or "dees" A and B. Since, according to the diagram, protons at d are pushed upward, the electric force there must be directed from B to A.

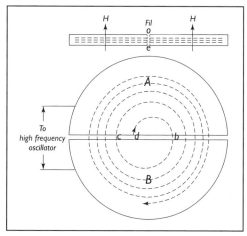

A diagram of the cyclotron principle published by Ernest Lawrence in 1932. The narrow horizontal box at the top shows a section through the space in which the protons spiral out from their origin in the filament at the center. H signifies the magnetic field.

Within A they feel no electric force (the dees act the part of drift tubes), but they are subject to a strong magnetic force perpendicular to the plane of their orbit. This bends their paths into a circle within A. When they return to the space between the dees at b, a radio-frequency oscillator has reversed the polarity: in traversing the gap, they are now pushed downward. This acceleration causes them to move in a wider circle in B under the constant magnetic force; owing to the nature of magnetic forces, the particles travel through the wider circle in B in the same time that they took to navigate the narrower one in A. When they return to the gap at c, the electric force has again switched polarity; another acceleration ensues; and the protons gradually spiral out to the circumference of the machine. In the 1930s, the energy that could be accumulated on a hydrogen nucleus was limited only by the size and expense of the magnet that forced the particles into spiral orbits. The biggest cyclotron magnet completed before World War II—the machine in which uranium first was transmuted into neptunium—weighed 2,000 tons.

text continued from page 115

Journalists came to the Cavendish wanting to know when physicists would be able to extract useful energy from atoms. "Never," Rutherford replied. The nucleus would always be a sink, not a source, of energy. No doubt in making this precipitous judgment he had the method, as well as the time and money, employed by Cockcroft and Walton too firmly and freshly in mind. In 1933 Rutherford brought this pessimistic view to a wider public in a long address over radio, which had become big business during the previous decade owing in large measure to advances made in military communication in the Great War. He observed that although the energy liberated in splitting a lithium nucleus is over 500 times that carried by the proton that strikes it, more than a thousand million protons must be fired for every effective hit. Only if disintegrating atoms prompted the transmutation of their neighbors could a chain reaction releasing useful amounts of energy occur. But, as Rutherford observed, that obviously does not happen. "If [it did] we should long ago have had a gigantic explosion in our laboratories with no one remaining to tell the tale."

But the Cavendish method of splitting atoms did cause a slow explosion 5,000 miles away. When he heard the news, Lawrence had already pushed protons to higher energies in his cyclotron than the Cavendish could reach with its machine. But like Cockcroft and Walton, Lawrence and his associates preferred to tinker with their apparatus than to look for disintegration. After the Berkeley laboratory received the news about the transmutation of lithium it took them six months to intensify the cyclotron's beam enough to confirm it. Meanwhile Lawrence had in hand a new and bigger cyclotron. Fowler and Cockcroft came to see it in 1933. They were not impressed. "Probably only trivial stuff," Fowler reported to Rutherford. "We can get in long before California," Cockcroft reassured Walton.

Lawrence generously offered to teach the Cavendish how to make a cyclotron and told Rutherford where to get parts cheaply. But the illustrious old Cavendish did not choose to be advised by upstarts from California. Although Chadwick wanted to explore the possibility of a cyclotron, Rutherford and Cockcroft elected to stay with the direct method of high potential that had proved itself so well. That was a mistake. Chadwick left the Cavendish in 1935 in order to have the freedom to build a cyclotron and, no doubt, to do other things. The following year Rutherford at last decided to authorize one and to raise the large sum of money by then required. He had no choice if the Cavendish was to remain at the forefront of nuclear physics. By 1936 the cyclotron had become the accelerator of choice, with energies far higher, and yields far greater, than cheaper machines could produce. The delay put the Cavendish two generations of accelerators behind Berkeley at the end of World War II.

The passing of the lead in experimental nuclear physics to Berkeley marked the definitive shift from the simple

Ernest Lawrence (left) and his graduate student Stanley Livingston stand beside the first major Berkeley cyclotron during its construction in 1932. The metal horseshoe frame and the metal cylinders beneath it create the magnetic field that controls the orbits of the spiraling particles. The vacuum chamber in which the particles move is shown with its lid removed in front of Lawrence. Half a dozen men could stand under the frame when the cylinders were removed.

sophistication of Rutherford's methods to the large and complicated engineering productions of California. At the same time, the small-team approach as practiced in the Cavendish, typically a collaboration of two or three people, gave way to work in interdisciplinary groups that might consist of chemists, physicists, medical doctors, and engineers. Rutherford had the singular fortune to preside over research and discovery in radioactivity and nuclear physics throughout the period that one man could hold the entire field in his head and operate all the instruments with his own hands. He had the quickness of intellect, boldness of conception, and vigor of body to discover not only a vast quantity of detail, but also fundamental truths about the nature of matter and the constitution of atoms, and to guide others to discoveries equally deep if not so plentiful.

In 1931 Rutherford was created a peer (a member of the British House of Lords). He took the name "Baron Rutherford of Nelson" and, for his arms, the unique design with its references to New Zealand and to the behavior of thorium and thorium X. The individual on the left of the arms is supposed to represent Hermes Trismegistus, "the thrice great Hermes," the grandfather of all alchemists; and the slogan at the base, *"primordia quaerere rerum,"* "to inquire into the foundations of things," defines Rutherford's career. His first speech as a baron in the House of Lords concerned a fundamental problem of practical transmutation: the transformation of coal, which Britain had in abundance, into oil, which it imported at great cost.

The additional prestige conferred by his baronetcy made Rutherford an ideal choice for figurehead in one of the great philanthropic undertakings of his time. This was the Academic Assistance Council, established in May 1933 to assist Jewish and other scholars discharged from their positions by the Nazi government of Germany. At first, pleading overwork and yielding to pressure from his wife, Rutherford declined the office. But as the Council's organizers talked to

him, "he exploded with wrath at Hitler's treatment of scientific colleagues whom he knew intimately and valued. He
would have been miserable if we [the organizers] went
ahead without him. He did everything and more to make
our going ahead possible." So Lord Beveridge, one of the
chief organizers, remembered Rutherford's recruitment.
With his help, the Council secured an administrative center
at the Royal Society.

The rescue was prompt and effective. Of the 650 teach-
ers and researchers discharged during the first two years
after the promulgation of the law for the "cleansing of the
civil service" (the staff of German universities were government employees), 57 found permanent academic employment in Britain, and 155 received temporary appointments;
many of these went on to long-term jobs in the United
States and elsewhere. Of the remaining 450, most found
employment in France and other European countries, the
British Commonwealth, the Americas, and Turkey.

Most of the Germans mentioned so far were not Jews
and did not emigrate. Planck sheltered Jews in the institutions over which he presided and tried to convince Hitler
that the measures against the civil service would destroy
German science; Hitler answered that he had nothing
against Jews, only against Communists, but unfortunately all
Jews were Communists. Then he flew into a rage so violent
that Planck had to creep away. Laue took part in mild
protests against the Nazi regime but otherwise stayed out of
sight. Geiger and Hahn retained their positions and worked
on the exploitation of nuclear energy during the war.
Hevesy, who had become a professor in Germany, made his
way to Copenhagen and settled in Sweden. Einstein, the
most prominent Jewish intellectual in Germany, was at
Caltech in Pasadena when the Nazis came to power. From
that safe distance he condemned Hitler's regime. He never
returned to Germany. A few months after the foundation of
the Academic Assistance Council, Einstein told a mass

meeting over which Rutherford presided that, as free men, they had the obligation to "save mankind and its spiritual acquisitions," to "save Europe from a new disaster."

Things only grew worse: people exempted from the first cleansing by the Nazis fell victim to later rounds. By 1936 Rutherford could report that the Council had assisted some 1,300 Germans, of whom 363 scholars had been re-established in appropriate positions around the world and 324 held temporary posts. The situation reached its nadir in 1938 with the joining of Germany and Austria and an alliance between Hitler and Mussolini, which extended the reach of the racial laws. That December Fermi, the greatest physicist in Italy, took his family to Sweden to see him receive his Nobel prize. His wife had Jewish blood. They left Stockholm not for Rome but for New York. Rutherford occasionally intervened in cases directly—for example, in favor of the daughter of Heinrich Hertz, whose work on radio waves had oriented his first steps toward science. His biggest case did not concern refugees from Nazi Germany, however, but a victim of another dictatorship, the Soviet Union.

Although urged repeatedly to become a British subject, Kapitsa had retained his Russian citizenship. In 1934 he returned to the Soviet Union to attend a scientific meeting and enjoy a vacation. The Kremlin refused to allow him to leave. He had been abroad long enough, it said, and his country now needed the scientific and technical knowledge he possessed. He protested and sulked, but to no avail. Rutherford led a long campaign to pressure Stalin to release Kapitsa. The Soviet embassy in London dismissed the effort with a well-aimed shot at the center of English science. "Cambridge would no doubt like to have all the world's greatest scientists in its laboratories in much the same way as the Soviet [Union] would like to have Lord Rutherford." Against the Soviet insistence that the country "urgently needs all her scientists" Rutherford's contention that kidnapping Kapitsa violated academic freedom and undermined international scientific relations could not prevail. Eventually Kapitsa made his peace with Stalin. Rutherford agreed to sell the Soviet Union whatever equipment Kapitsa needed from his laboratory at the Cavendish and the Soviet authorities established an institute of physics for him.

The deterioration of conditions in Europe brought the prospect of another world war. This time British scientists would not be caught unprepared. Already in the mid–1930s they began a program that resulted in the invention of radar and the construction of early warning stations just in time to greet the Luftwaffe, the German air force, when Hitler turned his attention to Britain in 1940. Rutherford advised the committee, chaired by one of his protégés, that had sponsored the radar program. In the last year of his life he urged the foundation of a Research Council to coordinate the scientific needs of the military services. But getting the army, navy, and air force to cooperate required a war, not a Rutherford, and he was no more successful in uniting the services than he had been in freeing Kapitsa.

On October 19, 1937, at the height of his prestige and power and in perfect health, Rutherford died from a preventable problem. He had suffered for some time from a small hernia, which he did not bother to have repaired. It strangulated as a result of some unusual exercise. He was violently ill. An emergency operation conducted by a London specialist seemed to correct the evil; but he had, in effect, poisoned himself, and he died four days after his accident of what the doctors called "intestinal paralysis." A great international meeting of scientists was then underway in Bologna to celebrate the 200th anniversary of the birth of Luigi Galvani, whose discoveries had prompted the invention of the battery and the birth of the electrical age. Lady Rutherford telegraphed the news to Bohr, who was one of the principal speakers at the centennial. Bohr tearfully announced the death of his old friend and advisor.

Rutherford has appeared on the stamps of several countries. The Soviet Union honored him in 1971, the centennial of his birth, with this head-and-shoulders portrait alongside a diagram of the theory of alpha scattering by the nuclear atom.

Rutherford received the greatest honor available to an Englishman. His ashes are buried in Westminster Abbey, where the remains of the most illustrious scientists and poets lie with those of kings. J. J. Thomson read the service. The High Commissioner of New Zealand, the Vice Chancellor of the University of Cambridge, the president of the Royal Society, and high officials of McGill University, Trinity College, and the DSIR, acting as pallbearers, represented the institutions that promoted his rise from poverty and obscurity to fame and power.

Lord Rutherford rests near Sir Isaac Newton, who set down the laws by which planets circle their suns, comets fly through the universe, moons draw tides, and apples fall to earth. Rutherford and his coworkers found a similar world in the atom. Newton devoted much of his life trying to make sense of alchemical recipes for the transmutation of metals. Rutherford established that nature itself is an alchemist and can transmute metals into gases and back again into solids. He managed to play the alchemist himself, with rays from radium and the beams from a particle accelerator.

Rutherford continued to accrue honors after he joined Newton in Westminster Abbey. One of the leading physics laboratories in England bears his name; four countries have issued postage stamps in his honor; and New Zealand, knowing his value, has put his face on its hundred-dollar bill. The most fitting memorial is a place in the periodic table. Element 104, made in a cyclotron at Berkeley by bombarding the world's supply of californium, has the unlikely name "rutherfordium." It is a heavier analog of hafnium (element 72), whose properties Bohr had predicted from his version of Rutherford's atomic model. Unlike hafnium, however, rutherfordium does not exist unless man makes it. It has a half-life of only 70 seconds and no natural parent. At the moment there may not be a single atom of it in the entire universe. Like Rutherford himself, it represents the ultimate in the alchemist's art.

1871

Born to James Rutherford, a flax farmer, and Maria Thompson Rutherford, a school teacher, near Nelson, New Zealand

1886

Enters Nelson College (a secondary school with 80 students) on a scholarship

1889–94

Attends Canterbury College (post secondary), also on scholarships; earns a bachelor's degree in 1892, a master's in 1893, and a bachelor's degree in science, with research on radio waves, in 1894

1895–98

Research at the Cavendish Laboratory, Cambridge, England, under (and with) J. J. Thomson; switches from radio waves first to X rays and next to radioactivity, both then brand-new fields

1898

Takes up professorship at McGill University, Montreal, Canada

1900

Discovers the emanation and active deposit of thorium

1901

Returns to New Zealand to marry Mary Newton

1902

With Frederick Soddy, plots the rise and decay curves for thorium X and devises the theory of radioactive disintegration and the transmutation of atoms; on his own, demonstrates that alpha rays are particles

1904

Publishes first edition of *Radioactivity*

1907

Becomes professor and director of the physics institute at the University of Manchester

1908

Begins experiments with Hans Geiger on counting alpha particles; demonstrates, with Thomas Royds, that alpha particles are helium ions; receives Nobel prize in chemistry

1910–11

Invents the nuclear atom

1912

Niels Bohr arrives in Rutherford's laboratory

1913

Bohr publishes his quantum theory of the atom; several of Rutherford's students put forward the concept of isotope

1913–14

Henry Moseley confirms concept of atomic number; Rutherford is knighted

1915

Rutherford's students rush to war, on both sides; Moseley is killed at Galipoli

1915–18

Rutherford helps organize British science for war; studies problem of submarine detection

1917

Heads a delegation of British and French scientists to the United States to discuss mobilization of American science

1919

Acomplishes and explains the artificial disintegration of nitrogen by alpha particles; J. J. Thomson retires from the Cavendish professorship

1920

Succeeds Thomson in Cambridge, begins to rebuild powerful research school

1922

Peter Kapitsa arrives at the Cavendish, joins James Chadwick, John Cockroft, and Patrick Blackett

1925

Rutherford receives Order of Merit from King George V

1926-31

Serves as president of the Royal Society

1931

Is made a life peer, takes the title Baron Rutherford of Nelson

1932

Chadwick discovers the neutron; Cockcroft and E. T. S Walton accomplish the first disintegration of a nucleus with particles accelerated by a machine

1933–37

Rutherford heads Academic Assistance Council to rescue academics fired by the Nazis

1936

Commissions a cyclotron for the Cavendish

1937

Dies suddenly, in otherwise good health, of a strangulated hernia

Terms in italics
are also defined
in the glossary.

Active deposit
The solid material left by the decay of *emanation.*

Alpha ray/particle
First detected as a constituent of *uranium rays,* later recognized
to be the helium *nucleus.*

Artificial radioactivity
Radioactivity acquired through a *nuclear reaction* provoked by a
nuclear scientist.

Atomic number
The charge on the *nucleus.*

Atomic structure
The arrangement of the *electrons* in an atom.

Atomic weight
The relative weight of an atom in multiples of the weight of a
hydrogen atom.

Beryllium rays
Neutrons.

Beta ray/particle
First detected as a constituent of uranium rays, later recognized
to be an *electron.*

Cathode ray
Supposed agent of the *fluorescence* of the glass of an evacuated
discharge tube, later recognized to be a stream of *electrons.*

Corpuscle
The universal constituent of matter according to J. J. Thomson,
later recognized to be an *electron.*

Cosmic rays
Streams of particles entering the atmosphere from beyond the
earth.

Cyclotron
A device for accelerating charged particles to high energies in
a spiral path.

Electrode
A metal fitting through which electricity enters or leaves a discharge tube or electrolytic cell or battery.

Electron

An elementary constituent of matter carrying the unit charge of electricity.

e/m

The ratio of a particle's charge to its mass.

Element

A chemically distinct substance not decomposable by chemical means.

Emanation

Radioactive gas given off in the natural decay of heavy radioactive elements.

Fission

The splitting of a heavy *nucleus* into two parts of roughly equal atomic weight.

Fluorescence

A glow of certain materials when bombarded by light or swift sub-microscopic particles.

Gamma rays

High energy X rays given off by *radioactive* substances.

Gas discharge

The passing of current between *electrodes* in a normally insulating gas.

Inert gas

A member of the argon (or "noble") family of gases, which ordinarily do not participate in chemical reactions.

Ion

An atom or molecule with a net electric charge.

Ionization

The process of creating *ions*.

Isotope

One of several atoms with the same atomic number and different *atomic* weight.

n/A

The ratio of the number of electrons in an atom to its atomic weight.

Neutron

A neutral particle with a weight approximately that of a proton.

Nuclear reaction

The result of the absorption of an elementary particle by a nucleus, usually designated by (α, p), (α, n), (γ, p), etc., indicating the nature of the incoming particle (in these cases alpha, alpha, and gamma) and the outgoing particle (proton, neutron, proton).

Nucleus

The positively charged center of an atom, very small in comparison with the volume occupied by the atom's electronic structure.

Proton

The *nucleus* of a hydrogen atom.

Quantum condition

A limitation on the mechanical behavior of a physical system arising solely from the existence of the *quantum* of action.

Quantum jump

The transition of an electron between two *stationary states.*

Quantum of action (h)

The minimum value of "action" (defined as the product of an energy by the time it acts or of a momentum by the distance it acts through) that can be exchanged in nature.

Radioactivity

The property of emitting *alpha, beta,* and/or *gamma rays.*

Radioelement

An element possessing *radioactivity.*

Stationary states

In Bohr's theory of the atom, orbits satisfying the *quantum condition* in which electrons can move without radiating.

Uranium rays

The rays from uranium that gave rise to the discovery of *radioactivity;* they consist of *alpha, beta,* and *gamma rays.*

X ray

An electromagnetic disturbance like light, but of much higher frequency.

PERIODIC TABLE

IA	IIA	IIIB	IVB	VB	VIB	VIIB	VIIIB	VIIIB	VIIIB	IB	IIB	IIIA	IVA	VA	VIA	VIIA	VIIIA
1 **H** 1.00794																	2 **He** 4.00260
3 **Li** 6.941	4 **Be** 9.01218											5 **B** 10.811	6 **C** 12.011	7 **N** 14.0674	8 **O** 15.9994	9 **F** 18.99840	10 **Ne** 20.1797
11 **Na** 22.98977	12 **Mg** 24.3050											13 **Al** 26.98154	14 **Si** 28.0855	15 **P** 30.97376	16 **S** 32.066	17 **Cl** 35.4527	18 **Ar** 39.948
19 **K** 39.0983	20 **Ca** 40.078	21 **Sc** 44.95591	22 **Ti** 47.88	23 **V** 50.9415	24 **Cr** 51.996	25 **Mn** 54.9380	26 **Fe** 55.847	27 **Co** 58.9320	28 **Ni** 58.6934	29 **Cu** 63.546	30 **Zn** 65.39	31 **Ga** 69.723	32 **Ge** 72.61	33 **As** 74.92159	34 **Se** 78.96	35 **Br** 79.904	36 **Kr** 83.80
37 **Rb** 85.4678	38 **Sr** 87.62	39 **Y** 88.90585	40 **Zr** 91.224	41 **Nb** 92.90638	42 **Mo** 95.94	43 **Tc** 98.9072	44 **Ru** 101.07	45 **Rh** 102.90550	46 **Pd** 106.42	47 **Ag** 107.8682	48 **Cd** 112.411	49 **In** 114.82	50 **Sn** 118.710	51 **Sb** 121.76	52 **Te** 121.757	53 **I** 126.09447	54 **Xe** 131.29
55 **Cs** 132.90543	56 **Ba** 137.327	57 **La** 138.9055	72 **Hf** 178.49	73 **Ta** 180.9479	74 **W** 183.85	75 **Re** 186.207	76 **Os** 190.2	77 **Ir** 192.22	78 **Pt** 195.08	79 **Au** 196.96654	80 **Hg** 200.59	81 **Tl** 204.3833	82 **Pb** 207.2	83 **Bi** 208.98037	84 **Po** 208.9824	85 **At** 209.9871	86 **Rn** 222.0176
87 **Fr** 223.0197	88 **Ra** 226.0254	89 **Ac** 227.0278	104 **Rf** 261.11	105 **Db** 262.114	106 **Sg** 263.118	107 **Bh** 262.12	108 **Hs** (265)	109 **Mt** (266)	110 **Uun** (269)	111 **Uuu** (272)	112 **Uub** ?						

58 **Ce** 140.115	59 **Pr** 140.90765	60 **Nd** 144.24	61 **Pm** 144.9127	62 **Sm** 150.36	63 **Eu** 151.965	64 **Gd** 157.25	65 **Tb** 158.92534	66 **Dy** 162.50	67 **Ho** 164.93032	68 **Er** 167.26	69 **Tm** 168.93421	70 **Yb** 173.04	71 **Lu** 174.967
90 **Th** 222.0381	91 **Pa** 223.0359	92 **U** 238.0289	93 **Np** 237.0482	94 **Pu** 244.0642	95 **Am** 243.0614	96 **Cm** 247.0703	97 **Bk** 247.0703	98 **Cf** 251.0796	99 **Es** 252.083	100 **Fm** 257.0951	101 **Md** 258.10	102 **No** 259.1009	103 **Lr** 262.11

The modern periodic table of the elements. The secondary block underneath the main table indicates "transition series," the rare earths analyzed by Moseley (from Cerium, Z = 58, to Lutecium, Z = 71) and their analogues from Thorium, Z = 90, to Lawrencium, Z = 103. The main series has been carried to Z = 112, named "uno-uno-bium," that is, "one-one-twoium;" apparently chemists have run out of people and places to install in the table.

General

Crowther, J. G. *The Cavendish Laboratory, 1874–1974*. New York: Science History, 1974.

Goldsmith, Maurice. *Frédéric Joliot-Curie*. London: Lawrence and Wishart, 1976.

Hackmann, Willem. *Seek and Strike. Sonar, Anti-Submarine Warfare and the Royal Navy, 1914–1954*. London: HMSO, 1984.

Heilbron, John, and Robert W. Seidel. *Lawrence and His Laboratory*. Berkeley: University of California Press, 1989.

Hendry, John. *Cambridge Physics in the Thirties*. Bristol: Adam Hilger, 1984.

Kevles, Daniel J. *The Physicists*. Cambridge: Harvard University Press, 1995.

Nye, Mary Jo. *Before Big Science: The Pursuit of Modern Chemistry and Physics*. New York: Twayne, 1996.

Stwertka, Albert. *A Guide to the Elements*, 2nd ed. New York: Oxford University Press, 2002.

Rutherford

Badash, Lawrence, ed. *Rutherford and Boltwood: Letters on Radioactivity*. New Haven: Yale University Press, 1969.

———. *Kapitsa, Rutherford, and the Kremlin*. New Haven: Yale University Press, 1985.

Bunge, Mario, and W. R. Shea, eds. *Rutherford and Physics at the Turn of the Century*. New York: Science History, 1979.

Campbell, John. *Rutherford: Scientist Supreme*. Christ Church, New Zealand: AAS Publications, 1999.

Eve, A. S. *Rutherford*. Cambridge: Cambridge University Press, 1939.

Feather, Norman. *Lord Rutherford*. London: Priority Press, 1973.

Wilson, David. *Rutherford: Simple Genius*. Cambridge, Mass.: MIT Press, 1984.

Colleagues and Coworkers

Brown, Andrew. *The Neutron and the Bomb: A Biography of Sir James Chadwick.* New York: Oxford University Press, 1997.

Hahn, Otto. *A Scientific Biography.* New York: Scribners, 1966.

———. *My Life.* New York: Herder and Herder, 1970.

Hartcup, Guy, and T. E. Alibone. *Cockcroft and the Atom.* Bristol: Adam Hilger, 1984.

Heilbron, J. L. *H. G. J. Moseley.* Berkeley: University of California Press, 1974.

Levi, Hilde. *George de Hevesy.* Copenhagen: Rhodos, 1985.

Merricks, Linda. *The World Made New: Frederick Soddy, Science, Politics, and Environment.* New York: Oxford University Press, 1996.

Moore, Ruth. *Niels Bohr.* New York: Knopf, 1966.

Pais, Abraham. *Niels Bohr's Times: In Physics, Philosophy, and Polity.* New York: Oxford University Press, 1991.

Parry, Albert. *Peter Kapitsa on Life and Science.* New York: Macmillan, 1968.

Pasachoff, Naomi. *Marie Curie And the Science of Radioactivity.* New York: Oxford University Press, 1996.

Quinn, Susan. *Marie Curie.* New York: Simon and Schuster, 1995.

Rayleigh, Lord. *The Life of Sir J. J. Thomson.* Cambridge: Cambridge University Press, 1942.

Rayner-Canham, Marlene F. and Geoffrey W. Raynar-Canham. *Harriet Brooks.* Montreal: McGill-Queens University Press, 1992.

Thomson, George P. *J. J. Thomson and the Cavendish Laboratory in His Day.* Garden City, N.Y.: Doubleday, 1965.

Thomson, J. J. *Recollections and Reflections.* New York: Macmillan, 1937.

ACKNOWLEDGMENTS

I thank Owen Gingerich for entrusting Rutherford to me, Nancy Toff for keeping me near the desired level, and Nancy Hirsch for procuring many of the figures.

J. L. Heilbron, formerly professor of history at the University of California at Berkeley and now a senior research fellow at Worcester College, Oxford, is the author of more than 20 books. His most recent titles include *Geometry Civilized* and *The Sun in the Church: Cathedrals as Solar Observatories.* He is also the editor of the *Oxford Companion to the History of Modern Science.*

Owen Gingerich is Professor of Astronomy and of the History of Science at the Harvard-Smithsonian Center for Astrophysics in Cambridge, Massachusetts. The author of more than 400 articles and reviews, he has also written *The Great Copernicus Chase and Other Adventures in Astronomical History* and *The Eye of Heaven: Ptolomy, Copernicus, Kepler.*